Primera edición: septiembre de 2023.

Copyright © 2023: José Alberto Ruiz Martínez (autor).

Equipo de creatividad, diseño y marketing: José García Ruiz (co(   )-, ∪ella
Morales Pérez (diseño y formato), Lidia María García Soler (diseño   ∪-), Jaime Zarco Dolz del
Castellar.

Marca registrada © Opospills, oposiciones con cerebro.

Título: **OPOSICIONES INGLÉS PRIMARIA. ¿Cómo elaborar una programación y una situación de aprendizaje de 10?**

ISBN (Papel): 9798859638888

Curricular elements

Context

Methodology planned

8 STEPS TO ELABORATE YOUR TEACHING PROGRAMME

Didactic units

Rest of the elements

Annexes

Evaluation process

Bibliography & references

8 STEPS TO ELABORATE YOUR TEACHING PROGRAMME

To elaborate a comprehensive and effective teaching programme for Primary Education we can follow a bottom-up analysis where, after learning the education legislation and the curricular elements, we can take into account multiple sources of information and perspectives to ensure that this teaching programme is comprehensive and tailored to the specific needs of the students and school. Therefore, the next steps can be considered:

1. Analyse the curricular elements

Check out the education legislation and school documents to identify the objectives of the stage and the school, key competences, specific competences of the area, evaluation criteria, and basic knowledge for the age group you are going to work with.

All of these elements should be based on the curricular development for our Primary stage (Royal Decree 157/2022 and subsequent development in the different Autonomous Communities)

2. Determine the context

It is essential to have a clear understanding of the school, the class you have selected, the students, their characteristics, and their needs.

This analysis should take into account the principles of inclusivity and diversity. The school educational project, as a document that provides information on the context in which the school operates, is a good source to find the socio-economic and cultural characteristics of the area, the needs of the students, and the resources available to the school

Teaching Programme
8 steps for it's elaboration

3. Plan the methodology

Decide on the teaching and learning strategies that will be used, taking into account the characteristics of the students, their needs, and their learning styles.

Determine the measures to cater for diversity, the resources needed, and any school plans, projects, or programmes that will be incorporated into the teaching programme

4. Sequence and develop the didactic units

Establish the time for each didactic unit and then design each one of them. Units may contain specific objectives and the rest of curricular elements. Plan this units keeping in mind the students' age and needs, the natural process of language acquisition (Krashen), and Bloom's taxonomy for the development of sequenced and structured activities

5. Establish the evaluation process

Determine the types of evaluation, procedures, and instruments that will be used to evaluate the students' learning. Also, consider the evaluation of the teaching practice to ensure continuous improvement

6. Prepare the annexes

Include (if you are allowed) or prepare (for your oral presentation) any additional materials, such as worksheets, posters, games, flashcards, etc., or any other relevant documentation

7. Compile the bibliography and references

Identify and compile the bibliography and references that will be used as a basis for the teaching programme

Teaching Programme
8 steps for it's elaboration

8. Write the rest of the teaching programme

Draft the elements of the teaching programme in an orderly and sequential manner. Remember to follow the specification or recommendations from the legislation in your Autonomous Community

BIBLIOGRAPHICAL REFERENCES & QUOTATIONS:

- Nunan, D. (1988). The learner-centred curriculum. Cambridge University Press.

- Nunan, D. (2003). Practical English language teaching. McGraw-Hill.

- Nunan, D. (2004). Task-based language teaching. Cambridge University Press.

> "The best curriculum is one that is learner-centred, meaningful, and relevant to the real-world needs and interests of students..

> "Good language teaching is not simply a matter of selecting and presenting suitable materials. It is also a matter of devising learning tasks that lead to the development of communicative competence".

- Marzano, R. J., Pickering, D. J., & Pollock, J. E. (2001). Classroom instruction that works: Research-based strategies for increasing student achievement. ASCD

> "Curriculum development is a dynamic, continuous, and ongoing process that is influenced by the nature and needs of the students, the skills of teachers, and the community in which learning takes place".

> "Effective planning is the key to successful instruction. Planning helps teachers anticipate potential problems and ensure that instruction is appropriate for all students. Planning also allows teachers to link instruction to learning goals, to determine what materials and resources are needed, and to prepare for effective delivery of instruction".

Teaching Programme
Bibliographical references & quotations

- Richards, J. C. (2001). Curriculum development in language teaching. Cambridge University Press.

- Richards, J. C., & Rodgers, T. S. (2014). Approaches and methods in language teaching. Cambridge University Press

> "The best curriculum is one that is learner-centred, meaningful, and relevant to the real-world needs and interests of students..

> "Good language teaching is not simply a matter of selecting and presenting suitable materials. It is also a matter of devising learning tasks that lead to the development of communicative competence".

- Brown, H. D. (2007). Teaching by principles: An interactive approach to language pedagogy. Pearson Education

> "The basic purpose of curriculum development and course planning is to provide direction and focus for teaching and learning activities, and to ensure that the instructional goals of the program are being met".

- Larsen-Freeman, D. (2018). Research in language teaching: Exploring socialization, identity, and agency. Routledge

> "Curriculum is like a road map for a journey, indicating where one is going and how to get there. But just as there are many ways to travel from one place to another, so too there are many ways to teach a subject".

> "Effective methodology involves a combination of different approaches and techniques, selected and adapted to meet the needs of individual learners and the goals of the course".

> "The physical arrangement of the classroom can have a significant impact on the learning experience. A well-designed classroom can facilitate communication, collaboration, and engagement among learners".

- Harmer, J. (2015). The practice of English language teaching. Pearson Education Limited.

> "Lesson planning is central to any successful teaching, and for new teachers it can be the most challenging aspect of the job".

DOCUMENT FOR THE ELABORATION

OF THE TEACHING PROGRAMME

PART 1

The present document tries to provide some guidelines for the orientation, elaboration and development of the Teaching Programme and the Didactic Units with its corresponding Learning Situations as described in the **Royal Decree 157/2022**, establishing the Minimum Teaching Requirements for the Primary Education. In order to do so, we shall start by introducing some important definitions.

1. CONCEPT OF CURRICULUM

In the **article 6** of the Organic Law 3/2020, of 30th December, of Modification of the Organic Law 2/2006 of Education (**LOMLOE**) the *curriculum* is defined as *"the set of objectives, competences, contents, pedagogical methods, and evaluation criteria of each of the education stages"*. Likewise, the **Royal Decree 157/2022**, March 1st, establishing the Minimum Teaching Requirements for the Primary Education, gives the same definition in its **article 11**, adding that **contents** will be expressed in the form of basic knowledge. So, there is no big change in terms of curriculum definition.

In the **article 2** of this Royal **Decree 157/2022** we also find the definition of each one of the elements of the curriculum, which are:

a) Objectives: achievements that students are expected to have attained by the end of the stage which are linked to the acquisition of key competences.

b) Key competences: skills that are considered essential for students to be able to progress with guarantees of success in their educational career. The key competences are included in the learner exit profile at the end of basic education and are the adaptation to the Spanish Education System of the key competences established in the Recommendation of the Council of the European Union of 22 May 2018 on key competences for lifelong learning.

c) Specific competences: performances that students must be able to perform in activities or situations whose approach requires the basic knowledge of each area or field. The specific competences constitute an element of connection between, on the one hand, the learner's exit profile and, on the other, the basic knowledge of the areas and the evaluation criteria.

d) Evaluation criteria: references that indicate the levels of performance expected of students in the situations or activities to which the specific competences of each area refer at a given moment in their learning process.

e) Basic knowledge: knowledge, skills and attitudes that constitute the contents of an area and which learning is necessary for the acquisition of the specific competences.

f) Learning situations: situations and activities that involve the students' development of actions associated with key competences and specific competences that contribute to the acquisition and development of these competences.

2. LEVELS OF SPECIFICATION

The curriculum must therefore be further specified by means of different levels of specification:

❑ **First Level** The official *curriculum* for the whole national territory (Royal Decree 157/2022) derives from the aims of education established in the Organic Law on Education (LOMLOE 3/2020) but focusing only on the characteristics and needs of the students in the Primary Education stage. This basic curriculum is further specified by each **Autonomous Community** with administrative competence in education matters, due to the government decentralization, which develops its own regional curriculum in accordance to the characteristics of the area (Decree, Order, etc.).

❑ **Second Level** Each *school* has also the **autonomy** and responsibility to adapt this regional curriculum to its own features and needs. Thus, as it is stated in article 120, section 2, of LOE 2/2006, "schools will have the autonomy to draw up, approve and execute an *Education Project*, as well as the procedures for the organisation and running of the school". Within this document, the fundamental guidelines of the school are made explicit, as it gives the school a unique character and personality. Therefore, in this document we may find the identity signs, the general organisation of the school (discipline, coordination, communication, etc.), the aims and objectives, general curriculum specifications, actions and plans (Coexistence, Tutorial, Reading, Health, Digital, ...), etc. which must be updated and included in the *Annual General Programme* every academic year.

❑ **Third Level** In each school, the teaching staff has also the responsibility to elaborate their teaching action plan through the *Teaching Programme* of each of the subjects from the curriculum. In our case, as FL teachers, the plan for every level where we teach the Foreign Language subject.

3. TEACHING PROGRAMME

According to **F. Imbernón (1992),** programming may be understood as "the establishment of a series of activities or tasks in a given context and timing in order to implement and teach some content so that certain objectives or goals may be attained."

The Teaching Programme is the document containing a set of decisions that allow us to carry out our work for **a specific group of students** in each particular Educational level for a given school year. It should be planned in an orderly and sequenced way, assuring the continuity of the learning and skills acquired in previous years, and setting the bases for the following levels.

The teaching programme is the document that should answer the following **questions**:

- **what, how** and **when** to teach?
- **What, how** and **when** to evaluate?

According to **Mariel Piqueres (2022)**, in education we do not work with products, but with people. That is why we must be aware that our profession is vocational and that it requires time, commitment, dedication, and patience. Spending **time** with our students includes not only work in the classroom, but also the creation of a good tool to make the journey as safe and organised as possible, taking into account the diversity of the passengers.

Therefore, this didactic or teaching programme should gather all the information and documentation prepared for a school year and for a specific subject, within a specific level or cycle of the educational stage. It should be the **reference** not only for teachers, but for the whole educational community.

The school's teaching staff, in the exercise of their autonomy and with the guidance of the educational administration, must reach agreements in **coordination** with all colleagues in the school for the elaboration of didactic programme models that meet the needs and characteristics of the institution and the students. These models are obviously open and flexible so that they can be tweaked and worked by every teacher in accordance with their respective subjects. Following these specifications, we may suggest the next outline for the elaboration of the Teaching Programme:

1. Introduction

1.1. Justification

1.2. Contextualisation: school and class

2. Curricular elements

2.1. Stage objectives (and school specific objectives)

2.2. Key competences. Exit profile (Operative Descriptors)

2.3. Specific competences of the area

2.4. Evaluation criteria

2.5. Basic knowledge (contents)

3. Methodology

3.1. Methodological implications

3.2. Measures to cater for diversity

3.3. Resources: material, human and spatial resources

3.4. School plans, projects and programmes

3.5. Complementary activities

4. Evaluation

4.1. Types of evaluation

4.2. Evaluation procedures and instruments

4.3. Evaluation of the teaching practice

5. Didactic Units

Unit 1: XXX

Unit ...

6. Bibliography and references

7. Annexes

Whatever option you decide to choose as an outline for the elaboration of your Teaching Programme, my recommendation is that you follow the next **steps**:

a) After a careful and thorough reading of the curriculum in your Autonomous Community, choose a specific level of Primary Education (age, number of students, ACNEAE, school and family context, possible interests and needs, etc.). Ideally, you may choose the one where you feel more comfortable, or you are more aware of the type of activities and tasks those students will need according to their characteristics. Write your first text for the contextualization of the school and class selected (ANNEX 1. SCHOOL & CLASS CONTEXT). You can focus on a school you know to help you get some ideas from their School Educational Project, the type of students and their characteristics, the families, facilities and resources, timetable, etc. Or you can invent the type of school community out of your imagination.

b) Start from the planning and development of the Teaching Units and their subsequent Learning Situations (remember that in a unit we may find 1 or more learning situations). We are going to start from the house foundations, not the roof. These will give you a general idea to elaborate and complete the rest of the parts of the Teaching Programme accordingly. Follow these **steps**:

b.1. Choose first the methodology you are going to use for the implementation of the learning situations and strategies or resources needed based on the basic knowledge for the specific year group (ANNEX 2. DRAFT OF FIRST IDEAS). Sometimes we can select more than one methodology or even some strategies that can be combined with that methodology (*e.g. Gamification can be part of a Project or Task-based learning methodology. Flipped classroom seems to be more appropriate for older students*).

b.2. Once we know the methodology intended, we can decide on the topics or titles to be covered in each unit in order to work the elements of the curriculum. We can start to plan some ideas or a draft for learning situations that may suit our students' characteristics and needs. You can include some **SDG** (Agenda 2030) as part of your learning situations to work some of the challenges our society is facing and maybe find solutions. So, we can start finding or identifying possible situations that our students may be interested in. Then, we continue justifying why we choose them and how we are going to work them with the description of the outcome intended, the final task. Some examples of final tasks are: oral presentation, video, email, lapbook, dramatization, campaign, debate, school event, etc. (Remember that with LOMLOE there has been a shift from a content-based to a **competency-based approach for learning**). Some examples could be:

We noticed that most of our students like to eat too many sweets around the days of Halloween. We want to work on a unit about this popular festivity to make our students aware of the pitfalls of consuming too many sugary or unhealthy products. We are going to develop a learning situation, within the unit of "Halloween", where the students will learn the amount of sugar and fat in these products and campaign against unhealthy habits to make the rest of the school and the families aware of other possible options to give as treats in those days.

We have seen that many of our students play and exchange Pokémon cards during playtime. We want to make use of the motivation that this game brings to our students with special needs. We have decided to develop a learning situation to work some vocabulary about parts of the body where the students will create their own Pokémon and play games that imply descriptions (adjectives, verbs, etc.) as well as computation (adding and subtracting numbers, etc.).

Try to be original with the topics and titles you choose for the units and learning situations, avoiding some like: "The family", "My body", "Animals", etc. In these cases, for instance, we could name these situations **"Frankie wants carrots"** and **"The Pokémon challenge"**.

Some examples of possible titles or ideas of teaching units or learning situations that can be worked in the FL classroom are:

Summer camp (Introducing yourself)

The new kid in the class (Pretending someone new comes, what would you say about you?)

A water leak in my house (Parts of the house. How can we build a house that gives us shelter?)

Ready, steady, go! (Parts of the body. Health. How can we take care of our own body for a race?)

I lost my pet! (Going to the park. What would you do if you lose your dog/cat/...?)

Together it's more fun! (Playing games. Rules, follow instructions, respect, is it fair to lose?)

A gift from granny (Birthday. What would you ask as a present to your granny/mum/dad/...? Why?)

It's freezing! (Clothes. Drama. What should you wear in different weather conditions?)

Master Chef (Food. What recipe would you do if you go to a food TV conquest?)

Pedro Pepperoni! (Food. How would you order some food? Phone call – Online – etc.)

Feeding the chickens (Animals. What do animals need to live? And humans?)

Don't get rid of it! (Objects. What would you do with your old toys or something to recycle?)

A special trip (Where would you like to go on holidays? What would you take with you? ...)

Etc.

Try to be coherent with your selection and maybe even follow a common **thread** or topic.

b.3. When you have the titles and number of units you need for your Teaching Programme, if you have not done so before, start with the timing of these units to have an idea on **how many sessions** you may need for each one (ANNEX 2. DRAFT OF FIRST IDEAS). This is really important to know how long each unit will take. Plan your units for this year or for the next school academic year (check the requirements from your Autonomous Community competitive exam guidelines).

Use a calendar and count 2/3 **sessions** per week (depending on the level selected and specifications from your regional organization of the Curriculum). You may follow a template like this for your timing:

FIRST TERM		
Teaching Unit	Lessons	Timing
1 Welcome back to school!	7	September 11th – October 6th
2 Spooky Halloween	6	October 9th – October 31st
3 Pokémon challenge	8	November 2nd – November 28th
4 ...		

Be aware that there are some units that may require just few lessons (such as those worked in "Halloween", "Christmas" or "Easter" time), whereas other units may require more time for their development. Sometimes, you can even integrate those sociocultural contents of special occasions or celebrations within a bigger didactic unit.

b.4. Once we have the general idea of what is going to be our plan for the whole year (methodology, topics we want to work, and how long we will devote to each one), then we can start with a draft of ideas of the activities and tasks for each lesson. When you are planning your sessions, remember that it is very important to keep in mind the **basic knowledge**, the **specific competences**, and the **evaluation criteria** from the Curriculum.

The normal structure of a lesson in a FL class is:

Warm-up	5 – 10 minutes	Preparing the context for learning.
Development	30 – 45 minutes	Demonstration, evaluation, practice, interaction, cooperation, creation, ...
Plenary or closing	5 – 10 minutes	Revision and consolidation.

The type and range of strategies or activities in each one of those sections is very diverse. Among them we may consider the following options:

WARM-UP	5-10 minutes

- o **KWL chart** (Know, Want to know, Learned): Students fill out with the teacher the first 2 sections (what they already KNOW about the topic, and what they WANT to know about that topic).
- o Starter sentence or **Tweet of the day**: ¨*Good morning class, today ...*¨
- o **Word of the day**: Write on a small poster or board the word of the day.
- o Short **video** about something already studied to engage the students in the class.
- o Singing a previously learned **song**.
- o **Show and tell**: Show a picture and ask the students to describe it.
- o **Hints**: Hide a picture and give some hints to the students to guess what it is.
- o **What's in the box/bag**? Students make questions to guess what it is.
- o **20/10 Questions** Teacher or 1 students think of a word, the rest have to guess asking questions.
- o **Secret word**: Give some hints, jumble the letters, put it reverse, etc.
- o **Make a sentence** with words: Students will try to make a sentence using as many words as they can from a list (e.g. I , my, go, then, am, because, etc.)
- o **Correct the spelling** of a word or grammar in a sentence (noticing).
- o **Starter cards**: Choose one card and make a sentence. Cards may include: Feelings (Today I am/feel ...), short sentence (I like..., Today I ..., Yesterday I..., etc.), links to start a sentence (First, Then, Later, After, Next, Finally, etc.)
- o Etc.

DEVELOPMENT (Starting – Practice – Consolidation)	30-45 minutes

SESSION 1 and successive sessions where you introduce contents
- **Starting**: Introduction/presentation/eliciting new concepts (introducing vocabulary):
  Songs
  Videos (e.g., https://youtu.be/FdILsxR5AE0)
  Stories, news, articles, texts, ...
  Flashcards (e.g., https://youtu.be/X9KebTgfLJI)
  Realia (real objects)
  Pre-evaluation (the teacher checks for comprehension and adjust the lesson accordingly)
- **Practice** of those concepts: (first teacher-controlled for demonstration, then students-led for participation and social interaction)

Demonstration: The teacher develops an action, or the teacher chooses some student/s to perform the action. The students see the intended activity or task.

IWB activities: for example: http://www.learningchocolate.com/

Worksheets (wordsearch, fill in the gaps, answer questions, matching, order words/pictures, etc.)

Games (guessing, matching, answering questions, moving, acting, ...)

Role-playing (the students take the role of another person: waiter, shop assistant, policeman, ...)

Dramatization (the students take the role of fiction characters: the wolf, the pigs, ...)

Simulation (the students act as themselves to perform a proposed situation in the classroom)

Songs with actions

Class Survey (example: favourite animal/food/sport/...)

Interview/questionnaire/...

Readings (books, articles, news, etc.) following a pre-, while- and post-activity with a purpose.

Tasks (short activities worked in cooperative work in pairs or small groups to achieve a common goal: explaining something, presenting, showing, etc. to solve a problem proposed)

Project work (big task carried out through some sessions in small groups to present an outcome: planning, sharing, monitoring, assessing, providing feedback, presenting, interacting, etc. with the goal of changing something, convincing someone, learning something new, etc.)

- **Consolidation** (mostly student-centred/student-controlled)

Questions and Answers with a communicative purpose or aim

Problem-solving tasks (ex: gathering information and presenting to the rest of the class)

Games (communicative games where they use the language learned)

Songs (the students are able to perform/sing the song by themselves)

Dictation (the students draw/glue/locate/write following the teacher's instructions)

Writing or recording a book, mini-book or comic (e.g. https://www.mystorybook.com), a letter, an email, postcard, invitation, ... to a friend/relative with a clear purpose.

Performing a play

Presentation of students' project/task to the rest of classmates

Discussions/Debates using the linguistic knowledge of the FL

OTHER EXAMPLES OF STRATEGIES USED IN THE SESSIONS COULD BE:

SESSION __ based on a ´story´

- Story related to the topic

Pre-, While-, and Post- Listening activities:

Questions/Predictions/Experiences

Worksheets (questions, complete the info, match, tick, number, sequence, etc.)

Creating a new end to the story

Unjumble the parts of the story (put in order pictures/words/dialogues)

Dramatization (the students turn to perform the story)

An example could be:

https://www.youtube.com/watch?v=SMy7mqjaWNc

SESSION __ focusing on ´phonemic awareness´ (Spelling and Pronunciation)

- Phonics

Spelling (specific sounds in words, for example: short and long vowel sounds as in mat, mate, sheep, ship, ... beginning sound as in shoes, socks, think, that, tricky words, etc.) You should bear in mind that this should be done in a progression from simple to more complex depending on the age and level of the students.

http://www.phonicsplay.co.uk/freeIndex.htm

http://jollylearning.co.uk/overview-about-jolly-phonics/

http://www.letters-and-sounds.com/what-is-letters-and-sounds.html

http://www.teachyourmonstertoread.com/

SESSION __ working some ICTs: use of computers or new technologies
- ICT lesson: website, CD/DVD, writing a letter/e-mail/essay/description/book, reading news/article, games (Kahoot!, Edpuzzle, Quiz Kit, Fanstasyclass, Plickers, etc.)
See: https://www.youtube.com/watch?v=ulb4jl3xqs8

SESSION __ working on CLIL: relationship with other subjects of the curriculum or SDG
- CLIL lesson: Social or Natural Science, Mathematics, Arts, PE, etc.
See: https://www.youtube.com/watch?v=uIRZWn7-x2Y
and a very good example: https://www.youtube.com/watch?v=dFuCrxRobh0

SESSION __ for revision
- Revision: If you run out of ideas to add in a lesson, you may consider doing one for revision.
If you plan a **flipped learning** lesson, you could include a session to consolidate what they worked at home making them share, interact, produce something, etc.

SESSION __ group work for the Final Task
- Work on Project/Final Task: Students gather in groups to work on their projects and use any kind of materials or resources they may need.

FINAL SESSION
- Present your Project to your classmates
- Final evaluation (written test, self-evaluation or reflection, Exit ticket, Language Portfolio, etc.)

PLENARY (closing of the lesson)	5-10 minutes

- o Plenary **cards**: Students pick one and complete the sentence (e.g. Today I have learned that ..., I need to practice more..., I enjoyed doing ..., I still don't understand ..., My favourite part ..., etc.).
- o Plenary **quiz** (questions about the topic studied) or Wheel of fortune quiz (a wheel with numbers or letters, each one correspond to a question: What was your favourite part today?, What did you learn today?, Teacher choice, etc.).
- o Short **video** about what has been studied (summary).
- o Singing the **song** previously learned.
- o **Think, pair, share**. Students think of 1 or 2 things they have learned in the lesson, then share.
- o **Bamboozle**. For quick revision. https://www.baamboozle.com
- o **Wordle**: As students say words they have learned; the teacher writes them down on the website: http://www.wordle.net/ and at the end you print it to post it on the wall.
- o **KWL chart** (Know, Want to know, Learned): Students fill out with the teacher the last part of the chart (what they have LEARNED in the unit) when the task is concluded.
- o **Exit ticket:** The students mark, colour or write how they value the lesson of the day, their implication and participation, the teacher and the resources, etc.
- o **Self-evaluation target:** Same as before but colouring a target divided in some parts as needed.

Keep in mind that these are just some ideas of possible exercises, activities, and tasks to be developed in the FL classroom. We must work towards the consecution of the development of the **key competences**; therefore, all of these strategies must be related to the **specific competences**, the **evaluation criteria** and the **operative descriptors** described in the curriculum.

During the process of planning the development of what it will give shape to the actual teaching units of your Teaching Programme you could jot down some notes of these **curricular elements** to be included later in the template of each one of them. Remember, they may be useful as a guide to choose activities, but they don't provide activities by themselves. That's why it is easier to start from the planning of activities and then select those curricular elements for each one.

So, it is advisable to start thinking of possible ideas for the development and final task of each unit, and from there plan the activities and strategies you are going to use following the intended methodology. This is the hardest part when doing a Teaching Programme, and the sooner you start with it, the more relaxed you will feel at the end of your teacher training. Besides, it is probably the part that takes longer, since you must look for a lot of resources, images, ideas, etc. or even create them.

You can use the model provided in the ANNEX 2. DRAFT OF FIRST IDEAS or the following template as a model to do this first draft. It is not the actual unit you will present in your Teaching Programme, since that one will include all the curricular elements, but it may help you sequence those activities in each lesson. As previously said, you can use this one or create your own one, whatever you think is going to help you better.

Year		Unit				
Learning situation				Timing		
Justification						
Outcome description						
LESSON PLAN						
Lesson	DEVELOPMENT				Scenarios	Resources
1	Warm-up: Development: Closing:					
2	Warm-up: Development: Closing:					
3	Warm-up: Development: Closing:					
4	Warm-up: Development: Closing:					
5	Warm-up: Development: Closing:					
6	Warm-up: Development: Closing:					
7	Warm-up: Development: Closing:					

An **example** of this first draft of ideas for the unit could be:

Year	3	Unit	1. Welcome back to school!		
Learning situation	New kid on the block!			Timing	1st Term – **7 lessons** Sept. 11th – Oct. 12th
Justification	Imagine we are going to have a new student coming to the classroom. He does not speak Spanish since he comes from an Eastern European country. However, he learned English at his previous school and even lived in England for a while. We want him to feel welcomed in our school.				
Outcome description	We want our students to introduce themselves and prepare as short presentation in their preferable format to show the new student our school and our community. The students will work in small groups of 4 to create their presentation and show their outcome as a final task.				

LESSON PLAN			
Lesson	DEVELOPMENT	Scenario	Resources
1	**Warm-up**: Tweet of the day! **Development**: Someone new Short video for introduction Game: Roll the dice and answer the question Classroom scavenger hunt (find something …) **Closing**: Exit ticket– What do you expect to learn this year?	Whole class Small heterogen. group	IWB Flashcards Big dice Chart
2	**Warm-up**: Starter cards **Development**: Who am I? Song to practice vocabulary Game: Guess who I am Role-play: Do you have _____? Can you _____? Task work: Initial meeting in groups to share ideas **Closing**: Plenary cards	Whole class Pairs Small heterogen. groups	IWB Cards game Plenary cards
3	**Warm-up**: Word of the day **Development**: This is my school Short introductory video and song Worksheet: Read and complete the text (school map) Task work: working on the design in groups **Closing**: Exit ticket- How did you do/feel today?	Whole class Pairs Small heterogen. groups	IWB Worksheet Exit ticket
4	**Warm-up**: Secret word **Development**: Where do you live? Short introductory video Game: Find in the map (locate parts of the neighbourhood) Task work: working and adding new things to their work **Closing**: Wheel of fortune Quiz game	Whole class Pairs Small heterogen. groups	IWB Map As needed from students
5	**Warm-up**: Show and tell **Development**: A special visit Visit from the local postman to tell us what he knows about the neighbourhood Task work: Working in groups to share and design ideas **Closing**: Exit ticket- What did you learn today?	Whole class Small heterogen. groups	IWB As needed from students
6	**Warm-up**: Starter cards **Development**: Rush hour! Short video of a child's daily routines in England Worksheet: Read and complete some questions (GRADED)	Whole class Small heterogen. groups	IWB Worksheet As needed from students

	Task work: working in groups to finalise their outcome **Closing**: Plenary cards		
7	**Warm-up**: Tweet of the day! **Development**: Show time! Few minutes in group to prepare their work **Task**: Short presentation of 5 minutes each group Feedback from partners and classmates **Closing**: Exit ticket- Self-reflection and evaluation	Whole class Small heterogen. Groups presenting	As needed for students' presentation Language Portfolio

The **actual teaching unit**, once you have all of your drafts of possible units to be developed, will include the **curricular elements** (as you will see in Part 2), as well as resources needed, possible link with other areas and SDG to be worked, how the unit is going to deal with diversity in relation to the UDL and cognitive styles from the pyramid in Bloom's taxonomy, and how you are going to cater with diversity in the case of having children with specific educational support needs. One **example** could be:

YEAR	3	UNIT		1. Welcome back to school!	
Learning Situation		New kid on the block!	TIMING	1st Term – **7 lessons** Sept. 11th – Oct. 12th	
Justification		Imagine we are going to have a new student coming to the classroom. He does not speak Spanish since he comes from an Eastern European country. However, he learned English at his previous school and even lived in England for a while. We want him to feel welcomed in our school.			
Description & Final task		We want our students to introduce themselves and prepare as short presentation in their preferable format to show the new student our school and our community. The students will work in small groups of 4 to create their presentation and show their outcome as a final task.			

Primary Stage Objectives	FL Basic knowledge
a) To know and appreciate the **values** and rules of **coexistence**, as well as the pluralism inherent in a democratic society. d) Know, understand and respect **different cultures** and differences between **people**, equal rights and opportunities for men and women and non-discrimination. f) To acquire in at least one **foreign language** the basic communicative competence that will enable them to express and understand simple messages and to cope in everyday situations.	**A. COMMUNICATION** - Self-confidence and reflection on learning. Error as an integral part of the process. - Basic communicative functions of common use appropriate to the setting and context: greeting, saying goodbye, introducing oneself and others; describing people, objects and places; asking for and exchanging information on everyday matters; describing routines. - Elementary vocabulary and vocabulary of interest to learners relating to close interpersonal relationships, housing, places and immediate surroundings.
Specific objectives	**B. PLURILINGUALISM** - Basic vocabulary and expressions for understanding statements about communication, language and learning (metalanguage).
1. Understand and produce very simple information about personal description. 2. Use different means of representation for communication and expression. 3. Respect the functional value of the foreign language and cultural diversity.	**C. INTERCULTURALITY** - The foreign language as a means of communication and relationship with people from other countries, and as a means of getting to know different cultures and ways of life.

FL Specific competences	Competence O.D.	Evaluation criteria
1. RECEPTION	CCL2 CP2	1.1 Recognise and understand words and expressions in short, simple oral, written, and multimodal texts.
2. PRODUCTION	CCL1 CPSAA5 CCEC4	2.3 Select and apply basic strategies to produce short, simple messages appropriate to communicative intentions, using physical or digital resources and support.
3. INTERACTION	CP1 CPSAA3	3.2 Select and use basic strategies for greeting, saying goodbye and introducing oneself; expressing simple, short messages; and asking and answering basic questions for communication.
4. MEDIATION	CP3 CPSAA1 CPSAA3	Understand and explain basic information about concepts, and short, simple texts in situations in which diversity must be catered for.
5. PLURILINGUALISM	CP2 CPSAA4 CPSAA5 CE3	5.2 Identify and apply knowledge and strategies to improve their ability to communicate and learn the FL, with the support of other learners and of analogue and digital media.
6. MULTICULTURALITY	CCL5 CPSAA1 CC2	6.1 Show interest in intercultural communication, identifying and analysing, with guidance, the most common discriminations, prejudices and stereotypes in everyday and common situations.

Link with other areas	SDG	UDL	Cognitive Styles
Natural & Social Science Arts Spanish Language & Lit.	Goal 4: Education Goal 5: Gender equality	Engage: Motivation act. Represent: Resources Express: Final product	LOTS: Explain & share ideas HOTS: Create & present

LESSONS: SEQUENCE OF COMPETENCES			
Lesson	ACTIVITIES	Scenario	Resources
1	**Warm-up**: Tweet of the day! **Development**: Someone new Short video for introduction Game: Roll the dice and answer the question Classroom scavenger hunt (find something …) **Closing**: Exit ticket– What do you expect to learn this year?	Whole class Small heterogen. group	IWB Flashcards Big dice Chart
2	**Warm-up**: Starter cards **Development**: Who am I? Song to practice vocabulary Game: Guess who I am Role-play: Do you have ____? Can you ____? Task work: Initial meeting in groups to share ideas **Closing**: Plenary cards	Whole class Pairs Small heterogen. groups	IWB Cards game Plenary cards
3	**Warm-up**: Word of the day **Development**: This is my school Short introductory video and song Worksheet: Read and complete the text (school map) Task work: working on the design in groups **Closing**: Exit ticket- How did you do/feel today?	Whole class Pairs Small heterogen. groups	IWB Worksheet Exit ticket

4	**Warm-up**: Secret word **Development**: Where do you live? Short introductory video Game: Find in the map (locate parts of the neighbourhood) Task work: working and adding new things to their work **Closing**: Wheel of fortune Quiz game	Whole class Pairs Small heterogen. groups	IWB Map As needed from students
5	**Warm-up**: Show and tell **Development**: A special visit Visit from the local postman to tell us what he knows about the neighbourhood Task work: Working in groups to share and design ideas **Closing**: Exit ticket- What did you learn today?	Whole class Small heterogen. groups	IWB As needed from students
6	**Warm-up**: Starter cards **Development**: Rush hour! Short video of a child's daily routines in England Worksheet: Read and complete some questions (GRADED) Task work: working in groups to finalise their outcome **Closing**: Plenary cards	Whole class Small heterogen. groups	IWB Worksheet As needed from students
7	**Warm-up**: Tweet of the day! **Development**: Show time! Few minutes in group to prepare their work **Task**: Short presentation of 5 minutes each group Feedback from partners and classmates **Closing**: Exit ticket- Self-reflection and evaluation	Whole class Small heterogen. Groups presenting	As needed for students' presentation Language Portfolio

MEASURES TO CATER TO DIVERSITY	
General measures	Specific measures
Groupwork Fast-finishers Graded tasks Different pace and rhythm	One-on-one intervention Curricular adaptation Individual intervention plan External support teacher

EVALUATION OF THE TEACHING PRACTICE						
Design	Appropriate methodology, activities, curricular elements, etc.	1	2	3	4	5
Implementation	Appropriate timing, cooperative work, diversity measures & eval. instruments	1	2	3	4	5

b.5. While you develop this first draft for the lessons for all your units, and the actual unit for your TP, make a revision to check out the **coherence** of those activities along the unit with the rest of aspects to be included. Do they make sense? Are they adapted to the students' interests, needs and characteristics? Have you considered measures to cater to diversity? (Heterogeneous groups, graded tasks and activities, extension work for fast finishers, etc.). Did you keep in mind the curricular elements? Are you going to follow the same thread? (Famous character, theme, movie, etc.). Also, while you work this units or learning situation, it is very helpful to create a booklet with some explanation of what you do in each lesson, showing some examples of worksheets, models for the games, story, photos, songs, etc. Something that is going to visually help the board of examiners understand what you do in only one page per session. Besides, this is going to catch their attention.

One **example** could be:

1. Get to know your teacher.

Good morning class. My name is Mrs. ...
I am your English teacher. I am ... years old.
My favourite food is spaghetti.

2. Game: Roll the dice to introduce yourself.

1. What's your name?
2. How old are you?
3. How many brother or sisters do you have?
4. What's your favourite food?
5. What's your favourite animal?
6. What's your favourite sport?

3. Classroom scavenger hunt: Find something ...

White   Blue   Big
        small
Yellow green
        long
        short

Jose A Ruiz
Teacher -Training Primary Education

DOCUMENT FOR THE ELABORATION
OF THE TEACHING PROGRAMME

PART 2

The development of a Teaching Programme is not as easy it might seem. In the first part of this document (Part 1) we provided some guidelines for its elaboration starting from the hardest and probably most difficult part, that is, finding, selecting, and planning the tasks and activities we are going to carry out along our lessons. The right selection of those tasks and activities needs to be in accordance with the specific level we select for our Teaching Programme, and therefore, we must not forget the students' age, interests, needs, etc.

We must also keep in mind that these tasks and activities worked throughout different learning situations must be relevant and connected to real life situations for the students, and they must foster the development of the competences as well, through the activation of the basic knowledge from the curriculum in resolution of challenges or problems related to the student's reality and their needs in a creative and cooperative way. For this reason, the right selection of the most appropriate methodology we are going to use is so important, in order to satisfy all of our students' needs and interest (following the **Universal Design for Learning** principles) and contribute to the development of those competences.

Once we have decided on the right selection of the methodology to follow, and we have planned our draft of ideas for our teaching units and learning situations, we can continue with the actual writing and development of the rest of the parts of this document that we will call ¨my Teaching Programme¨. But first, let's make a revision of those elements we want to include in this document, that is, the outline we propose as a final outcome.

1. Introduction

1.1. Justification

1.2. Contextualisation: school and class

2. Curricular elements

2.1. Stage objectives (and school specific objectives)

2.2. Key competences. Exit profile (Operative Descriptors)

2.3. Specific competences of the area

2.4. Evaluation criteria

2.5. Basic knowledge (contents)

3. Methodology

3.1. Methodological implications

3.2. Measures to cater for diversity

3.3. Resources: material, human and spatial resources

3.4. School plans, projects and programmes

3.5. Complementary activities

4. Evaluation

4.1. Types of evaluation

4.2. Evaluation procedures and instruments

4.3. Evaluation of the teaching practice

5. Didactic Units

Unit 1: XXX

Unit ...

6. Bibliography and references

7. Annexes

Following this outline, we should have already worked some parts devoted to the ¨introduction¨. This introduction is going to be divided into ¨**theoretical justification**¨ and ¨**contextualisation**¨. The former is going to make reference to the importance of the FL area in our Spanish Education System and make a connection with all the legislation documents for the elaboration of this Teaching Programme (levels of curricular specification). The latter is going to set the context where this programme is going to be implemented, that is, the school and the group of students selected (age, characteristics, etc.). I personally recommend doing 1 page for each one of these two parts (no more than 3 pages in total). Here you should not forget to mention some important aspects such as the ¨Education Project¨, the ¨Annual General Programme¨, some specific programmes developed in the school (Erasmus+), etc.

The next section we need to focus on is the development of the curricular elements, which can be extracted from the **Royal Decree 157/2022** or the curriculum from the education legislation of your Autonomous Community.

These curricular elements can be listed, and then we can make some connection among them whenever it is possible or necessary. It is important to point out that when we do each of these sections, we should start with a short introductory explanation to give an understanding of why we put them in our Teaching Programme. An example could be:

STAGE GENERAL OBJECTIVES

The **Royal Decree 157/2022** establishing the Primary Education Curriculum defines the objectives, in its **article 7**, as the reference to the achievement that the student must attain at the end of the educational process, as a result of the teaching and learning experiences intentionally planned for this purpose. These objectives (which are a reflection of the intentions and goals established in the law on education LOMLOE 3/2020) contribute to the development and achievement of the key competences, and they are defined as the skills and capabilities that the students must develop throughout this stage in order to enable them to:

a) know and appreciate the **values** and rules of **coexistence**, to learn to act in accordance with them in an empathetic way, to prepare for the active exercise of citizenship and to respect human rights, as well as the pluralism inherent in a democratic society.

b) develop **habits** of individual and **teamwork**, effort, and responsibility in their study, as well as attitudes of self-confidence, critical thinking, personal initiative, curiosity, interest, and creativity in learning, and entrepreneurial spirit.

c) acquire **skills** for the peaceful resolution of **conflicts** and the prevention of violence, which will enable them to develop autonomously in the school and family environment, as well as in the social groups with which they interact.

d) know, understand, and respect **different cultures** and differences between **people**, equal rights and opportunities for men and women and non-discrimination of people on grounds of ethnicity, sexual orientation or identity, religion or beliefs, disability or other conditions.

e) know and use appropriately the **Spanish language** and, if any, the co-official language of the Autonomous Community, and to develop reading habits.

f) acquire in at least one foreign language the basic communicative competence that will enable them to express and understand simple messages and to cope in everyday situations.

g) develop basic **mathematical competences** and begin to solve problems that require the performance of basic calculation operations, knowledge of geometry and estimation, as well as to be able to apply them to everyday life situations.

h) know the fundamental aspects of Natural **Sciences**, Social Sciences, **Geography**, **History** and **Culture**.

i) Develop basic **technological competences** and initiate in their use, for learning purposes, developing a critical mind towards their functioning and the messages they receive and elaborate.

j) Use different **artistic** representations and expressions and initiate in the construction of visual and audiovisual proposals.

k) Value hygiene and health, accept one's own body and that of others, respect differences and use **physical education**, sport and food as means to favour personal and social development.

l) Know and value the **animals** closest to human beings and adopt modes of behaviour that favour empathy and care for them.

m) develop their **affective capacities** in all areas of their **personality** and in their relationships with other people, as well as an attitude against violence, prejudices of any kind and sexist stereotypes.

n) develop daily habits of healthy autonomous active mobility, promoting **road safety** education and attitudes of respect that have an impact on the prevention of traffic accidents.

Apart from these Primary Education stage general objectives, in our Teaching Programme we can include some of the school general aims, or objectives, that we try to pursuit with our teaching practice in the specific context of the school where we work. These specific or school objectives are the ones expressed within the intentions of the School Educational Project. They usually mark the guidelines for the whole school community to work towards a common goal in relation to what it is supposed to be best for the school and the students' success by the end of their time in the school.

The stage **objectives** are closely linked to the **key competences**, as it is stated in the Royal Decree 157/2022. Then, through the attainment of those objectives all along the teaching and learning processes that take place in the FL area, we will contribute to the work and development of these key competences.

These key competences can be defined as expected knowledge, skills and attitudes needed by our students for their personal fulfilment and development in order to be able to solve real-life problems.

The learner Exit Profile at the end of basic education is the tool that specifies the principles and aims of the Spanish Education System in relation to basic education. This curricular element identifies the key competences that all students, without exception, must have acquired and developed by the end of compulsory education, first in Primary and later in Secondary.

The Exit Profile is the cornerstone of the curricular building, the matrix that unifies the different stages and modalities that make up the basic education of the Spanish Education System. It is therefore conceived as the element that should guide and underpin the rest of the curricular decisions, the strategies and methodological orientations in teaching practice and the element of reference for the internal and external assessment of students and their learning.

The Exit Profile is based on a structural and functional vision of the key competences, the acquisition of which is considered essential for the students' personal development to solve situations and problems in different areas of their lives.

RD 157/2022. Article 9. Key competences and Student Exit Profile at the end of Basic Education.

The key competences of the curriculum are:

(CCL) Competence in linguistic communication

(CP) Plurilingual competence

(STEM) Mathematical competence and competence in science, technology and engineering

(CD) Digital competence

(CPSAA) Personal, social and learning to learn competence

(CC) Citizenship competence

(CE) Entrepreneurial competence

(CCEC) Cultural awareness and expression competence

As regards to the applied dimension of the key competences, a set of operative descriptors has been defined for each of them, on the basis of the different existing European reference frameworks.

The operative descriptors of the key competences constitute, together with the objectives of the stage, the reference **framework** from which the specific competences of each area are specified.

SPECIFIC COMPETENCES OF THE FL AREA & OPERATIVE DESCRIPTORS

The specific competences of the FL area in Primary Education are, in many cases, the starting point for formal language learning. In Primary Education, the starting point is still a very basic stage of the FL, so that, throughout the whole stage, it will be essential to base learning on the repertoires and experiences of the pupils, thus facilitating their participation in simple acts of communication. This includes the implementation of communicative activities and strategies of **comprehension**, **production**, **interaction** and **mediation**, in line with the Action-oriented Approach suggested in the Common European Framework of Reference (CEFR-Companion Volume, 2020). These specific competences of the FL area also include fostering **plurilingualism** and appreciation of **linguistic**, **artistic**, and **cultural diversity** among pupils so that they learn to manage **intercultural** communicative situations.

The 6 specific competences of the FL area can be described in terms of "**what**" we want our students to achieve, "**how**" they could do it, and "**why**" it is important for them to develop these competences.

WHAT – HOW – WHY

The link between operative descriptors and specific competences makes it possible to infer from the **assessment** of these area competences the degree of acquisition of the **key competences** defined in the student's **exit profile**.

1. Understand the general meaning and specific information in short, simple texts, expressed clearly and in standard language, making use of a variety of strategies and using, when necessary, different types of support, in order to develop the linguistic repertoire and to respond to everyday communicative needs.
CCL2. Understand and evaluate simple oral, written, signed or multimodal texts in the personal, social and educational fields, with occasional support, in order to participate actively in everyday contexts and to construct knowledge.
CCL3. Locate, select and contrast, with appropriate support, simple information from two or more sources, evaluating its reliability and usefulness according to the reading objectives, and integrate and transform it into knowledge in order to communicate it, adopting a creative, critical and personal point of view while respecting intellectual property.
CP1. Use at least one language, in addition to the familiar language(s), to respond to simple and predictable communicative needs, in an appropriate way both in terms of development and interests and in everyday situations and contexts in the personal, social and educational fields.
CP2. Recognise, based on his/her experiences, the diversity of linguistic patterns, and experiment with strategies which, with guidance, enable him/her to make simple transfers between different languages in order to communicate in everyday contexts and extend his/her individual linguistic repertoire.

	STEM1. Use, with guidance, some inductive and deductive methods of mathematical reasoning in familiar situations, and select and use some strategies to solve problems, reflecting on the solutions obtained.
	CD1. Carry out guided research on the Internet and make use of simple strategies for the digital processing of information (key words, selection of relevant information, data organisation, etc.) with a critical attitude towards the contents obtained.
	CPSAA5. Plan short-term objectives, use self-regulated learning strategies and participate in self- and co-evaluation processes, recognising his/her limitations and knowing how to find help in the process of knowledge construction.
	CCEC2. Recognise and show interest in the peculiarities and intentions of the most outstanding artistic and cultural manifestations of heritage, identifying the media and formats, as well as the languages and technical elements that characterise them.

2. Produce simple texts in a comprehensible and structured way, using strategies such as planning or compensation, to express short messages related to immediate needs and to respond to everyday communicative situations.

	CCL1. Express facts, concepts, thoughts, opinions or feelings in oral, written, signed or multimodal form, with clarity and appropriateness to different everyday contexts of his/her environment, and participate in communicative interactions with a cooperative and respectful attitude, both to exchange information and create knowledge and to build personal bonds.
	CP1. Use at least one language, in addition to the familiar language(s), to respond to simple and predictable communicative needs, in an appropriate way and in everyday situations.
	CP2. Recognise, based on his/her experiences, the diversity of linguistic patterns, and experiment with strategies which, with guidance, enable him/her to make simple transfers between different languages to communicate in everyday contexts and extend his/her individual linguistic repertoire.
	STEM1. Use, with guidance, some inductive and deductive methods of mathematical reasoning in familiar situations, and select and use some strategies to solve problems, reflecting on the solutions obtained.
	CD2. Create, integrate and re-elaborate digital content in different formats (text, table, image, audio, video, software...) using different digital tools to express ideas, feelings and knowledge, respecting intellectual property and copyright of the content reused.
	CPSAA5. Plan short-term objectives, use self-regulated learning strategies and participate in self- and co-evaluation processes, recognising his/her limitations and knowing how to find help in the process of knowledge construction.
	CE1. Recognise needs and challenges to be faced and develop original ideas, using creative skills and being aware of the consequences and effects that the ideas could generate in the environment, to propose valuable solutions.
	CCEC4. Experiment creatively with different means and supports, and different plastic, visual, audiovisual, sound or body techniques, to elaborate artistic and cultural proposals.

3. Interact with other people using everyday expressions, making use of cooperative strategies and employing analogue and digital resources, to respond to immediate needs of their interest in respectful communicative exchanges.

	CCL5. Apply communicative practice at the service of democratic coexistence, the dialogical management of conflicts and the equal rights of all people, detecting discriminatory uses, as well as abuses of power, to favour not only the effective but also the ethical use of the different communication systems.

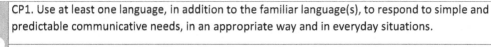	CP1. Use at least one language, in addition to the familiar language(s), to respond to simple and predictable communicative needs, in an appropriate way and in everyday situations.
	CP2. Recognise the diversity of linguistic patterns, and experiment with strategies which enable him/her to make simple transfers between different languages to communicate in everyday contexts and extend individual linguistic repertoire.
	STEM1. Use, with guidance, some inductive and deductive methods of mathematical reasoning in familiar situations, and select and use some strategies to solve problems, reflecting on the solutions obtained.
	CPSAA3. Recognise and respect other people's emotions and experiences, participate actively in group work, assume assigned individual responsibilities and use cooperative strategies aimed at achieving shared goals.
	CC3. Reflect and discuss current values and ethical issues, understanding the need to respect different cultures and beliefs, to care for the environment, to reject prejudices and stereotypes, and to oppose any form of discrimination or violence.
	CE1. Recognise needs and challenges to be faced and develop original ideas, using creative skills and being aware of the consequences and effects that the ideas could generate in the environment, to propose valuable solutions.
	CE3. Create original ideas and solutions, plan tasks, cooperate with others in teams, valuing the process carried out and the result obtained, in order to carry out an entrepreneurial initiative, considering the experience as an opportunity to learn.

4. Mediate in predictable situations, using strategies and knowledge to process and transmit basic and simple information in order to facilitate communication.

	CCL5. Apply communicative practice at the service of democratic coexistence, the dialogical management of conflicts and the equal rights of all people, detecting discriminatory uses, as well as abuses of power, to favour not only the effective but also the ethical use of the different communication systems.
	CP1. Use at least one language, in addition to the familiar language(s), to respond to simple and predictable communicative needs, in an appropriate way and in everyday situations.
	CP2. Recognise the diversity of linguistic patterns, and experiment with strategies which enable him/her to make simple transfers between different languages to communicate in everyday contexts and extend individual linguistic repertoire.
	CP3. Know and respect the linguistic and cultural diversity present in his/her surroundings, recognising and understanding its value as a factor of dialogue, in order to improve coexistence.
	STEM1. Use, with guidance, some inductive and deductive methods of mathematical reasoning in familiar situations, and select and use some strategies to solve problems, reflecting on the solutions obtained.
	CPSAA1. Be aware of own personal emotions, ideas and behaviours and use strategies to manage them in situations of tension or conflict, adapting to change and working to achieve own goals.
	CPSAA3. Recognise and respect other people's emotions and experiences, participate actively in group work, assume assigned individual responsibilities and use cooperative strategies aimed at achieving shared goals.
	CCEC1. Recognise and appreciate the fundamental aspects of cultural and artistic heritage, understanding the differences between cultures and the need to respect them.

5. Recognise and use personal linguistic previous knowledge across different languages, reflecting on how they work and identifying one's own strategies and knowledge, in order to improve one's response to specific communicative needs in familiar situations.

	CP2. Recognise the diversity of linguistic patterns, and experiment with strategies which enable him/her to make simple transfers between different languages to communicate in everyday contexts and extend individual linguistic repertoire.
	STEM1. Use, with guidance, some inductive and deductive methods of mathematical reasoning in familiar situations, and select and use some strategies to solve problems, reflecting on the solutions obtained.
	CD2. Create digital content in different formats using different digital tools to express ideas, feelings and knowledge, respecting copyright of the content used.
	CPSAA1. Be aware of own personal emotions, ideas and behaviours and use strategies to manage them in situations of tension or conflict, adapting to change and working to achieve own goals.
	CPSAA4. Recognise the value of effort and personal dedication for the improvement of his/her learning and adopt critical thinking in guided reflection processes.
	CPSAA5. Plan short-term objectives, use self-regulated learning strategies and participate in self- and co-evaluation processes, recognising his/her limitations and knowing how to find help in the process of knowledge construction.
	CE3. Create original ideas and solutions, plan tasks, cooperate with others in teams, valuing the process carried out and the result obtained, in order to carry out an entrepreneurial initiative, considering the experience as an opportunity to learn.

6. Appreciate and respect linguistic, cultural and artistic diversity from the foreign language, identifying and valuing the differences and similarities between languages and cultures, in order to learn to manage intercultural situations.

	CCL5. Apply communicative practice at the service of democratic coexistence, the dialogical management of conflicts and the equal rights of all people, detecting discriminatory uses, as well as abuses of power, to favour not only the effective but also the ethical use of the different communication systems.
	CP3. Know and respect the linguistic and cultural diversity present in his/her surroundings, recognising and understanding its value as a factor of dialogue, to improve coexistence.
	CPSAA1. Be aware of own personal emotions, ideas and behaviours and use strategies to manage them in situations of tension or conflict, adapting to change and working to achieve own goals.
	CPSAA3. Recognise and respect other people's emotions and experiences, participate actively in group work, assume assigned individual responsibilities and use cooperative strategies aimed at achieving shared goals.
	CC2. Participate in community activities, in decision-making and in the resolution of conflicts in a dialogic and respectful way with democratic procedures, the principles and values of the European Union and the Spanish Constitution, human rights, the value of diversity, and the achievement of gender equality, social cohesion and the Sustainable Development Goals.
	CC3. Reflect and discuss current values and ethical issues, understanding the need to respect different cultures and beliefs, to care for the environment, to reject prejudices and stereotypes, and to oppose any form of discrimination or violence.
	CCEC1. Recognise and appreciate the fundamental aspects of cultural and artistic heritage, understanding the differences between cultures and the need to respect them.

Therefore, in this table we can see how for each one of the specific competences of the FL area there are some correspondent operative descriptors that can be observed and measured for the evaluation of the students' development of the key competences. In order to evaluate the performance of these descriptors we can use some kind of **rating scale** to give a value from poor achievement to outstanding, either YES/NO, 1 to 10, or even 1 to 5, as we can see in the following chart:

OPERATIVE DESCRIPTOR EVALUATION				
1	2	3	4	5
Low	Below Average	Average	Above Average	Outstanding
The student shows low understanding and performance of the operative descriptor and needs some help.	The student shows understanding but is still in the process of achievement of the operative descriptor with some help.	The student shows understanding and starts to develop the operative descriptor with very little or no help.	The student shows very good understanding of the operative descriptor and acts autonomously.	The student shows excellent understanding of the operative descriptor, acts autonomously and helps others.

This rating scale can be used to assess the student's exit profile in a rubric as follow:

 RUBRIC FOR THE FL AREA STUDENT'S EXIT PROFILE

		CE.1	CE.2	CE.3	CE.4	CE.5	CE.6
CCL	CCL1						
	CCL2						
	CCL3						
	CCL4						
	CCL5						
CP	CP1						
	CP2						
	CP3						
STEM	STEM1						
	STEM2						
	STEM3						
	STEM4						
	STEM5						
CD	CD1						
	CD2						
	CD3						
	CD4						
	CD5						

	CPSAA1						
	CPSAA2						
	CPSAA3						
	CPSAA4						
CPSAA	CPSAA5						
	CC1						
	CC2						
	CC3						
CC	CC4						
	CE1						
	CE2						
	CE3						
CE	CE3						
	CCEC1						
	CCEC2						
	CCEC3						
CCEC	CCEC4						

This student's exit profile can be used as a tool for the evaluation of the student's development of the key competences along the academic year that s/he is attending. However, the value we provide to the achievement of each descriptor (extracted from the rating scale used) **can be changed** throughout the process of the same academic year or even in future academic years, and it cand be used as a reference for future teachers the student may have.

As stated in the **article 14** of the Royal Decree 157/2022, the evaluation of the students must be global, continuous and formative, and will take into account the degree of development of the key competences and their progress in the learning processes as a whole. Additionally, in the **article 25** it is described that the results of the evaluation shall be expressed in the following terms: "Insufficient (IN)", for negative marks and "Sufficient (SU)", "Good (BI)", ¨Notable (NT)¨and "Outstanding (SB)", for positive marks. Therefore, if we use a **rating scale** from **1 to 10**, for example, we must calculate the mean from the data obtained in the rubric adding all the scores and dividing by the number of criteria used. This way, we may use the same numeric score that represents these previous values, that is:

IN	SU	BI	NT	SB
1-5	5-6	6-7	7-9	9-10

In the case of having a **rating scale** of **1 to 5**, then we would need to do a bit more complicated process. So, we will need to add the total marks of the scores in the specific competences of each operative descriptor (N), multiply it by 10 and divide it by 30. Thus, we will obtain the weighted average with the result of each one of the operative descriptors (X).

$$X = N*10/30$$

The evaluation criteria, according to the **article 2** of the **RD 157/2022**, can be defined as "the reference that indicates the levels of performance expected by students in the situations or activities to which the specific competences of each area refer at a given moment in their learning process". Thus, these criteria determine the degree of acquisition of the specific competences by students and are therefore linked to them. They are formulated in terms of skills by stating the process or ability that students must acquire.

In the article 14 of the RD 157/2022 it is stated that "the assessment of students will be global, continuous and formative, and will take into account the degree of development of the key competences and their progress in the learning processes as a whole." ... "Likewise, the use of varied, diverse, accessible evaluation instruments adapted to the different learning situations that allow the objective assessment of all students will be promoted."

In the FL area, the evaluation criteria are based on the guidelines described in the Common European Framework of Reference for Languages (CEFR – Companion Volume) reformulated in 2020, and they must be adapted to the maturity and psychological development of pupils in Primary Education.

These evaluation criteria help us to better see and understand the degree of achievement of the operative descriptors of the students' exit profile. Therefore, they could be considered as specifications of these operative descriptors in relation to the FL area.

In the following chart we can see how for each specific competence of the FL area there is one or more evaluation criteria that are going to be used as a reference for the assessment of the degree of development of these specific competences, and which in turn are connected with the key competences through their operative descriptors.

Sp.Comp.1		Sp.Comp.2			Sp.Comp.3		Sp.Comp.4	Sp.Comp.5			Sp.Comp.6	
RECEPTION		PRODUCTION			INTERACTION		MEDIATION	PLURILINGUAL			MULTICULTURAL	
Ev.1.1	Ev.1.2	Ev.2.1	Ev.2.2	Ev.2.3	Ev.3.1	Ev.3.2	Ev.4	Ev.5.1	Ev.5.2	Ev.5.3	Ev.6.1	Ev.6.2
OP. DESCRIPT: CCL2, CCL3, CP1, CP2, STEM1, CD1, CPSAA5, CCEC2		OP. DESCRIPTOR: CCL1, CP1, CP2, STEM1, CD2, CPSAA5, CE1, CCEC4			OP. DESCRIPTOR: CCL5, CP1, CP2, STEM1, CPSAA3, CC3, CE1, CE3		OP. DESCRIPT: CCL5, CP1, CP2, CP3, STEM1, CPSAA1, CPSAA3, CCEC1	OP. DESCRIPT: CP2, STEM1, CD2, CPSAA1, CPSAA4, CPSAA5, CE3			OP. DESCRIPT: CCL5, CP3, CPSAA1, CPSAA3, CC2, CC3, CCEC1	

The evaluation criteria of each area are specifications based on the learning objectives established in the curriculum but with a major focus on the intended goals of the area. Therefore, they can be seen as smaller statements or breakdowns that are going to serve as the reference for the levels of performance expected by students in the situations or activities planned, to which the specific competences of the area refer at a given moment in their learning process. Thus, they provide a wider range of opportunities to observe and assess the students' learning and performance.

These evaluation criteria of each one of these FL specific competences and their correspondent operative descriptors can be seen in the following table:

SPECIFIC COMPETENCE	EVALUATION CRITERIA	OPERATIVE DESCRIPTOR
1. **Understand** the general meaning and specific information in short, simple texts, making use of a variety of strategies and using support, to develop the linguistic repertoire and to respond to everyday communicative needs.	1.1 Recognise and **understand** words and expressions in short, simple **oral**, **written**, and **multimodal** texts on familiar topics of personal relevance and close to the learner's own experience, expressed in a comprehensible, simple, and direct way, and in standard language.	CCL2 CCL3 CP1 CP2 STEM1 CD1 CPSAA5 CCEC2
	1.2 Select and apply in a guided way basic strategies in everyday communicative situations of relevance to the learner to **grasp the general idea** and identify specific elements with the help of linguistic and non-linguistic elements of the context.	
2. **Produce** simple texts in a comprehensible and structured way, using strategies such as planning or compensation, to express short messages related to immediate needs and to respond to everyday communicative situations.	2.1 **Express orally** short, simple sentences containing basic information on everyday topics, using verbal and non-verbal resources in a guided manner, using previously presented models and structures, and paying attention to **rhythm, stress and intonation.**	CCL1 CP1 CP2 STEM1 CD2 CPSAA5 CE1 CCEC4
	2.2 **Write** words, familiar expressions and phrases from models and with a specific purpose, using analogue and digital tools, using basic vocabulary and structures on everyday topics and those of personal relevance to the learner.	
	2.3 Select and apply, with guidance, basic **strategies** to **produce** short, simple **messages** appropriate to communicative intentions, **using**, with help, **physical** or **digital** resources and support depending on the needs of the moment.	
3. **Interact** with other **people** using everyday expressions, making use of cooperative strategies, and employing analogue and digital resources, to respond to immediate needs of their interest in respectful communicative exchanges.	3.1 **Participate**, with guidance, in basic **interactive situations** on everyday topics, prepared in advance, using a variety of media, relying on resources such as repetition, slow pace or non-verbal language, and showing empathy.	CCL5 CP1 CP2 STEM1 CPSAA3 CC3 CE1 CE3
	3.2 Select and **use**, with guidance and in familiar contexts, basic **strategies** for greeting, saying goodbye and introducing oneself; expressing simple, short messages; and asking and answering basic questions for communication.	

		CCL5
4. **Mediate** in predictable **situations**, using strategies and knowledge to process and transmit basic and simple information in order to facilitate communication.	Understand and explain, with guidance, basic information about concepts, communications, and short, simple texts in situations in which diversity must be catered for, showing empathy and interest in the interlocutors and in the problems of understanding in their immediate context, using a variety of resources and media.	CP1 CP2 CP3 STEM1 CPSAA1 CPSAA3 CCEC1
5. **Recognise** and **use** personal **linguistic previous knowledge** across different languages, reflecting on how they work and identifying one's own strategies and knowledge, to improve self-response to specific communicative needs in familiar situations.	5.1 **Compare** and contrast obvious **similarities** and **differences** between different **languages**, reflecting, with guidance, on basic aspects of how they work.	CP2 STEM1 CD2 CPSAA1 CPSAA4 CPSAA5 CE3
	5.2 **Identify** and **apply**, with guidance, **knowledge** and **strategies** to improve their ability to communicate and learn the FL, with the support of other learners and of analogue and digital media.	
	5.3 Identify and **explain**, with guidance, basic **progress** and difficulties in the process of learning a FL. (ex. Language Portfolio)	
6. **Appreciate** and **respect** linguistic, cultural and artistic **diversity** from the FL, identifying and valuing the differences and similarities between languages and cultures, in order to learn to manage intercultural situations.	6.1 Show **interest** in **intercultural communication**, identifying and analysing, with guidance, the most common discriminations, prejudices and stereotypes in everyday and common situations.	CCL5 CP3 CPSAA1 CPSAA3 CC2 CC3 CCEC1
	6.2 **Recognise** and **appreciate** the **linguistic** and **cultural diversity** related to the foreign language, showing interest in knowing its fundamental cultural and linguistic elements.	

As it is stated in the **article 2** of the **Royal Decree 157/2022**, the specific competences constitute an element of connection between, on the one hand, the learner's exit profile and, on the other, the basic knowledge of the areas and their evaluation criteria.

In any case, when we are planning a Teaching Programme for a specific group of students, we must keep in mind this specific content of the FL area that is going to equip the students with those tools and knowledge that is considered essential for the development of the specific competences related to the acquisition of the linguistic skills and understanding and respect of its culture. This basic knowledge is going to conform the type of activities we will plan to evaluate those competences.

The article 2 of the RD 157/2022 describes basic knowledge as the ¨knowledge, skills and attitudes that constitute the contents of an area and which learning is necessary for the acquisition of the specific competences¨.

The FL area helps students to face the challenges of the 21st century, helping them to acquire the basic knowledge necessary to start managing intercultural situations, democratic coexistence, dialogue-based conflict resolution and the establishment of personal and social bonds based on respect and equal rights. Thus, the Foreign Language area should favour empathy, develop curiosity for knowledge of other social and cultural realities and facilitate intercultural communicative competence based on the students' relationship with speakers of other languages, starting from a position of respect for the interlocutor, their customs and their culture.

Therefore, this basic knowledge combines the knowledge (knowing), skills (knowing how to do) and attitudes (knowing how to be) necessary for the acquisition of the specific competences of the area and favours the evaluation of learning through the criteria. They are structured in three **blocks**:

A. Communication, which covers the knowledge that needs to be mobilised for the development of communicative activities of comprehension, production, interaction and mediation.

B. Plurilingualism, which integrates the knowledge related to the ability to reflect on the functioning of languages in order to contribute to the learning of the foreign language and to the improvement of the languages that make up the linguistic repertoire of the pupils.

C. Interculturality, in which cultural knowledge is grouped together with its appreciation as an opportunity for enrichment and the development of attitudes of interest in knowing and understanding other languages, linguistic varieties and cultures.

Some Autonomous Communities have added a **fourth block** to this basic knowledge integrating the grammatical, discourse or functional content of the FL as well, such as expressions of time, space, existence, aspect, etc.

Students are expected to be able to put this basic knowledge into practice in communicative situations specific to the different fields: personal, social and educational; and on the basis of texts (either oral or written) on everyday topics of relevance to them that include aspects related to the Sustainable Development Goals (SDG) and the challenges of the 21st century. In line with the action-oriented approach of the CEFR-CV (2020), which contributes significantly to the design of active methodologies, the competency-based nature of the FL curriculum invites teachers to create interdisciplinary, contextualised, meaningful and relevant **tasks**, and to develop learning situations based on an integrated treatment of languages where learners are considered as progressively autonomous social agents and gradually responsible for their own learning process, and where their repertoires, interests and emotions, as well as their specific circumstances, are taken into account.

Some **examples** of these meaningful **learning situations** could be:

- Meeting someone new.
- Calling or answering someone on the phone, chat, etc.
- Crafting a card to a friend (Invitation, postcard, celebration, etc.)
- Helping someone to get somewhere or receiving and giving directions.
- Going to a doctor's appointment (or vet, dentist, company director, etc.)
- Going shopping, to a restaurant, to the park, the cinema, the zoo, a museum, an art gallery, etc.
- Doing an interview, filling an application form, questionnaire, survey, etc.
- Writing a letter, email, etc. to a relative, a friend, or pen pal.
- Creating a leaflet, pamphlet, publicity to make people aware of something.
- Participating in a debate to support certain ideas.
- Applying for a grant, job, etc.
- Making an experiment or device individually or in collaboration with partners.
- Etc.

As we can see, many of these tasks and activities that can be used in meaningful and contextualised learning situations can be done through **role plays**, some others require individual planning and elaboration or even group work discussion to reach an intended outcome. In this sense, we must be very clear about the methodology we are going to use to integrate all the prescriptive content or basic knowledge from the curriculum into a series of learning situations that are going to be contextualised and close to the students' reality in the form of previously planned learning situations. The selection of the right methodology and resources used to implement it, as well as the appropriate evaluation instruments selected will very much contribute to a well-functioning and development of our teaching programme.

Opospills

DOCUMENT FOR THE ELABORATION
OF THE TEACHING PROGRAMME

PART 3 The third part of this document, and following the outline previously presented, is going to be focused on the methodological implications for the elaboration, development and implementation of the Teaching Programme and some extra evaluation guidelines.

As we know, the main objective of the Foreign Language area in Primary Education is the acquisition of basic communicative competence in the FL, as well as the development and enrichment of pupils' intercultural awareness. Therefore, the core of the Foreign Language curriculum is crossed by the two dimensions of plurilingualism: the communicative and the intercultural dimension.

This area helps students to face the challenges of the 21st century, helping them to acquire the basic knowledge necessary to start managing future communicative situations, at the same time that enables pupils to become better prepared for digital environments and to get closer to the cultures conveyed by means of the FL learning. In this sense, digital tools have a potential that could be fully exploited to enhance the learning, teaching and assessment of foreign languages and cultures.

As we know, the Communicative Approach has been commonly used since the early 1980s as the paradigm for language instruction, however recent approaches (Piccardo & North, 2019) have evolved to expand and complement it, and one of them is the Action-oriented Approach.

The Common European Framework of Reference (Council of Europe, CEFR 2001 and CEFR-CV 2020) emphasises the importance of students' development of the communicative competence and integrates the new Action-oriented Approach as a complementary paradigm for language learning. In this new view, the CEFR describes language proficiency in terms of ¨what learners can do with the language¨ (i.e., their communicative competence) rather than ¨what they know about the language¨ (i.e., their linguistic competence).

The Action-oriented Approach (AoA) is based on the idea that languages are acquired through a process of interaction, communication and problem-solving. It is based on the constructivist learning theory that states that knowledge is built through experience, active engagement, and reflection. It is therefore a learner-centred approach that focuses on students as social agents that learn to use the target language as a tool for action and problem-solving, which is considered essential for their development.

In an action-oriented classroom, students are encouraged to take an active role in their learning, participating in tasks and projects that require the use of the target language in order to complete them. Those tasks are real-life and meaningful for the student, leading them to take initiative and make decisions in the target language.

This approach also emphasizes the need for students to use and apply the language in a natural context, this means that the language is not an end in itself but a means to an end, facilitating the student's interaction with the world. As a result, this approach aims to provide students with the opportunity to use the target language in real-life situations and to develop the skills they need to communicate effectively. As we can see, this can be a great complement to the communicative approach, which focuses more on the target language as a tool for communication rather than as a means to an end.

APPROACHES & METHODS IN FLT

It is important to mention that different approaches and methodologies may be used together and tailored to the specific students and context. The key is to find an approach that is effective and engaging for the students, and that promotes their progress in the target language. Among the different proposals that we currently have for second or foreign language acquisition we may highlight the following:

- ☐ **Content and Language Integrated Learning (CLIL):** CLIL is an approach where the FL is used as the medium of instruction for teaching non-language subjects, such as science, math, or social studies. This transversal approach for interdisciplinarity can provide students with the opportunity to learn content and language simultaneously, in a more authentic and meaningful context.

- ☐ **Task-based Language Teaching (TBLT):** This is an approach that emphasizes the use of communicative tasks as the primary means of language instruction. Students engage in tasks that are relevant and meaningful to them, such as planning a trip or giving a presentation. This approach encourages students to use the target language in a real-life context, and to develop the skills they need to communicate effectively.

- ☐ **Project-Based Learning (PBL):** PBL is an approach where students work on a project that is relevant to their interests and the curriculum (multidisciplinary). Projects can be completed in small groups, and can include activities such as research, writing, and presentation. PBL provides students with the opportunity to use the target language in a real-life context, and also encourages collaboration and problem-solving skills that can be connected sometimes to raise awareness on the Sustainable Development Goals (SDG) proposed by the United Nations.

- ☐ **Game-based Learning:** This approach uses games, puzzles, and interactive activities as a way to engage students and provide them with opportunities to practice the target language in a fun and dynamic way. Game-based learning can also be used to motivate students and make learning more enjoyable.

- ☐ **Blended Learning:** This approach combines online and offline resources and activities, such as interactive language-learning software, videos, and games, with traditional classroom instruction (as it is the case of "**flipped classroom**"). Blended learning can be great for differentiated instruction since it allows students to work at their own pace and to review material they have previously covered. It can also provide teachers with valuable insights into how their students are progressing and what areas need to be covered more in-depth.

These are a few examples of current practices in FL instruction in Primary Education, other modern methodologies that can be considered are **Gamification**, **Cooperative** Learning, **Problem Based** Learning, **Service-Learning** Projects, or Teaching Proficiency through Reading and Storytelling (**TPRS**), among others. The specific approach will depend on the school, the students, and the resources available, but the goal is always to create a positive, effective and real language learning experience for students.

According to the Communicative Approach and the Action-oriented Approach described in the Common European Framework of Reference for Languages (CEFR), the main methodological implications for foreign language teaching are as follows:

1. The focus must be set on the development of the communicative competence: The primary goal of language education should be the development of learners' communicative competence, which is their ability to use the language effectively in real-life situations. This should be the core of the curriculum, assessment, and teaching and learning practice.

2. The use of authentic and adapted materials to the language level: In order to provide learners with opportunities to use the language in real-life situations, authentic and real-like adapted materials and activities should be used as much as possible. This means using real or adapted texts, recordings, songs, games, and other materials that are similar to what native speakers would use in similar situations.

3. The use of communicative tasks and activities: Rather than focusing on the study of grammar or vocabulary in isolation, learners should be engaged in communicative tasks that require them to use the language to achieve specific communicative goals. This can include activities such as asking and giving directions, making reservations, visiting places or describing a picture. It also means using activities that simulate real-life communication, such as games, role-plays, simulations, and discussions.

4. Using a variety of teaching methods and strategies, such as individual, pair work, group work, and whole class activities, to cater to the different learning styles and needs of students. Also, incorporating technology and multimedia resources, such as interactive whiteboards, tablets, videos, and online games, to enhance students' engagement and motivation. Obviously, hands-on and manipulative resources would also benefit language exploration and use, especially with younger children.

5. The use of the target language as much as possible: In order to develop learners' ability to use the language effectively, the target language should be used as much as possible in the classroom. This means that the teacher and the students should speak the target language as much as possible in their interactions. Some programmes and projects can also be encouraging to favour the exchange of communication in real interaction with other English speakers and learners. For example, through Erasmus+ projects (KA2), eTwinning programmes, pen pal exchanges, etc.

6. The use of balanced implicit and explicit form-focused instruction: While the primary focus should be on communication, there is still a need to address grammatical aspects both implicitly and explicitly, especially when learners are facing difficulties in using the language correctly. This means that teachers may provide explicit instruction on grammar, vocabulary, and other linguistic features of the language, but in a way that is connected to the communicative activities and tasks. On the other hand, some strategies to teach grammar implicitly are "noticing", providing context to the text, etc.

7. The use of learner-centred approach: The learners should be seen as **active agents** in their own learning, and the teaching should be tailored to their needs and preferences. This means that teachers should provide learners with opportunities to take control of their own learning, and to make decisions about what, how, and when they will learn. This way, we are creating a positive and inclusive classroom environment to support students in their language learning journey.

8. Encouraging students to reflect on their own learning process and progress through peer feedback, self-reflection and evaluation, learning from mistakes, keeping track of learning in a journal or portfolio, etc.

Some of the elements that promoted the law LOE 2/2006 and continued being encouraged by LOMLOE 3/2020 is equity in education and attention to diversity. Being **diverse** is a condition inherent to human development: each student has his own different individual characteristics which will affect his learning process (different aptitudes, interests, cognitive styles, personality, prior knowledge and experience, motivation to learn, sociocultural background, among others). Thus, in this stage of Primary Education, and following the recommendations from the article 16 of the Royal Decree 157/2022, particular emphasis will be placed on paying attention to students' diversity for inclusion and quality education, by means of personalised and individual attention, early detection and prevention of learning difficulties, and putting into practice support and reinforcement mechanisms as soon as these difficulties are detected. We may be aware of the fact that pupils have different learning styles and provide the opportunity for each pupil to develop and fulfil their full potential according to their individual strengths, aptitudes and preferences.

The FL teacher may contribute to the development of the tutorial action plan through the orientation of the students' education process and the coordination with the rest of teachers, the intervention specialists, and the families. In addition, the law LOMLOE 3/2020, in its article 19 about Pedagogical Principles, state that *"flexible measurements and alternative methodologies in teaching and assessing the foreign language must be provided for students with specific educational support needs"* (ACNEAE). These reinforcement mechanisms, that must be put into practice as soon as learning difficulties are detected, may be both organizational and curricular. Thus, we will apply the most appropriate measures so that the assessment conditions are adapted to those students with special educational support needs. Among these measures we may consider the individual support, flexible groupings, reinforcement, use of graded-tasks or even curricular adaptations.

These measures must be included among the aims and strategies of the "Attention to Diversity Plan" from the schools and integrated into the Educational Project. In some cases, we may need to modify or adapt contents or methods so that every student can achieve the intended goals. In some others, we might need to offer extension activities for the fast-finisher students. Therefore, we must constantly address these issues, presenting the same activities in various ways and proposing other activities (reinforcement or expansion activities) that allow individual attention to students, as regarded among the guidelines of the Universal Design for Learning.

UNIVERSAL DESIGN FOR LEARNING

Universal Design for Learning (UDL) is an educational framework that aims to make instructional materials and environments more accessible to all students, including those with disabilities. The framework is based on three main principles: multiple means of **representation**, multiple means of **expression**, and multiple means of **engagement**. These principles are intended to provide students with different ways to access, engage with, and express their understanding of the material. UDL seeks to reduce barriers and increase opportunities for learning by providing a wide range of options for how students can learn, how they can demonstrate their learning, and how they can be engaged in the learning process. It obviously pays attention to the different learning styles and **multiple intelligences** (kinaesthetic, musical, mathematical, visual, linguistic, etc.) of students for learning (H. **Gardner**).

Some examples of UDL **strategies** that can be used in FL teaching and learning include:

A. Multiple means of representation: Using a variety of media, such as videos, audio recordings, images, and text, to present vocabulary and grammar concepts.

B. Multiple means of expression: Providing different ways for students to demonstrate their understanding of the material, such as through digital or analogue written texts, drawings, cooperative tasks, oral presentations, or audiovisual projects.

C. Multiple means of engagement: Creating interactive activities such as role-playing, games, and group discussions, etc., to engage students in the material and allow them to practice using the language.

UDL should be applied thoughtfully and in a way that is adapted to the needs of the specific students and the context of the class. It helps reduce barriers and increase opportunities for learning, and, in the case of FL learning, it favours the application of active learning methodologies such as task-based learning and content-based instruction.

Among the specific strategies and techniques which can be applied and implemented in the FL class following this UDL recommendations we may find:

- **Use of multimedia resources**: Incorporating 21st technology and multimedia resources, such as social media, images, videos and audio recordings, etc., to appeal to different learning styles and interests.

- **Use of first language**: Allowing students to use in a sensitive way their mother tongue as a support tool during the process of learning a second language.

- **Adaptive learning tools**: Using technology to provide personalized instruction and feedback, such as software that adjusts the difficulty level of exercises based on a student's performance.

- **Differentiated instruction**: Adapting the curriculum, teaching methods, and materials to meet the diverse needs and interests of students.

- **Scaffolding**: Providing support for students who are struggling, such as modelling, providing extra practice, and giving feedback on their work.

- **Flexible grouping**: Using different group dynamics, such as ability groups, interest groups, and mixed-ability groups, (homogeneous and heterogeneous groups), to support student learning.

- **Collaborative learning**: Encouraging students to work together in pairs or small groups, to enhance their language proficiency and communicative abilities.

- **Alternative assessment**: Offering multiple formats or ways for assessments, such as open-ended questions, performance tasks, projects, and self-reflection activities, to accommodate different learning styles and abilities.

UDL is an ongoing process and requires continuous adaptation and reflection. It is also important to note that UDL is not just about accommodating strategies for students with disabilities, it aims to improve the learning of all students, not just those with disabilities.

STUDENTS WITH SPECIFIC EDUCATIONAL SUPPORT NEEDS

Students with specific educational support needs (ACNEAE) are students who require additional support in order to access and engage in the curriculum. The article 71 of the law LOMLOE 3/2020, refers to these students as those *"who require educational attention different from the rest due to special education needs, developmental delay, language and communication development disorders, attention (ADHD) or learning disorders, severe lack of knowledge of the language of learning, or socio-educational vulnerability."*

The education administrations in each Autonomous Community usually provide some guidelines for the attention to students with specific educational support needs (ACNEAE). However, it is worth noting that the classification of these students may vary based on regional laws and specific education policies. My recommendation is that you read the legislative reference documents that regulate the attention to diversity in your Autonomous Community.

The title 2 of the law on education (LOE 2/2006 and LOMLOE 3/2020) devoted to the equity in education provides a different classification from previous years. Nevertheless, it still keeps the 3 main sections that establish the following categories:

1. Students with special education needs (SEN).

The article 73 of the law LOMLOE 3/2020 defines the students with special education needs (SEN) as ¨a student with SEN refers to be one who faces barriers that limit their access, presence, participation on learning derived from disabilities or serious behavioural, communication and language disorders, and who requires specific supports and educational attention to the achievement of the learning objectives. ¨

Intellectual disabilities: is significantly below average intellectual functioning present from birth or early infancy, causing limitations in the ability to conduct normal activities of daily living. It can be genetic or the result of a disorder that interferes with brain development. Some examples are fragile X syndrome, down syndrome, Angelman syndrome, developmental delay, etc. Some authors also include autism (TEA) within this group, but some others agree that this disorder should be part of an independent group.

Physical disabilities: it may be a genetic disorder or a serious injury at any time of a person's life. There are some types of physical disabilities, among others: brain injury, spinal cord injury, spina bifida, cerebral palsy, cystic fibrosis, multiple sclerosis and epilepsy.

Sensory impairment: it refers to the inability to interact with the world around us and other people. Sensory disabilities can involve any of the five senses, but for educational purposes, it generally refers to autism and a disability related to hearing, vision, or both hearing and vision.

Severe behaviour, communication and language disorders: it refers to the students with social emotional behaviour disorders and oppositional defiant disorder on the one hand, and severe speech and language impairment on the other hand. In this group we may find students with emotional, behavioural and mental disorders, such as anxiety, depression, or bipolar disorder.

Multiple disability: it refers to students with multiple disabilities, such as those with both physical and intellectual disabilities.

2. **High ability students or gifted and talented students.**

High ability students, also known as gifted and talented students, are those who have demonstrated exceptional abilities in academics, music and arts, or other areas. In Primary Education, these students may require specialized instruction or enrichment activities to challenge them and help them reach their full potential. This may include programmes such as advanced curriculum (normally providing content from two years ahead), accelerated instruction, extra or extended work, and mentoring. It is important for educators to identify and support high ability students to ensure they receive an education that is appropriately challenging and stimulating, however in Primary education more specific measures and diagnosis is not generally conducted until the 3rd level of the stage.

3. **Late entry students into the Spanish Education System.**

Late entry students refer to students who enter the Spanish education system later than the typical age at which students begin their studies. This can happen for a variety of reasons, such as immigration, family circumstances, or delays in the educational system due to a specific illness. These students may face additional challenges when starting their education, such as language barriers or gaps in their knowledge, but there are programmes and resources available to help them succeed, depending on the regional education administrations. In most cases, these students attend compensation for the education classes in the school ("compensatoria") to receive the help in language development from a support teacher.

4. **Students with specific learning difficulties.**

Under this category, we may find several groups of students with learning difficulties such as those who present difficulties in reading (dyslexia), writing (dysgraphia) and calculation (dyscalculia), as well as other categories such as ADHD, language specific disorder, non-verbal disorder, etc. Some authors may place here students with autism spectrum disorder (TEA) as well, due to the wide range that it covers.

There are some other learning difficulties that are not grouped or categorised within any group of students with specific educational support needs (ACNEAE) for not presenting any serious disability but still require some type of support in schools when they face any barrier in their learning process that may present a disadvantage. Among these, we may say those connected with speech problems: dyslalia, dysglossia, dysfemia, aphasia, dyspraxia, dysphagia, dysphonia, dysarthria, mutism, etc., and those due to adverse childhood experience, abuse, adverse social status, etc.

Summarising, it is important to note that these students (ACNEAE) may have different needs, and the support that works for one student may not work for another. In a student-centred approach, where the needs of each individual student are considered and a variety of strategies and resources are used to support the student, it is essential to consider these differences to provide the necessary support for each student. For that reason, in most cases early detection is essential, and the coordination with the psycho-pedagogical team and other specialists is important in order to develop the necessary individual and personalised action plan to cater to the specific needs of each individual.

In our case, the selection of appropriate materials and resources in the FL class can greatly enhance the learning experience for all students, but special attention must be paid into the right options for students with specific educational support needs in order to improve their chances of success. Using materials and resources that are tailored to their individual needs can make the learning process more accessible and effective for these students.

Chapter 2 from Title 5 of the law LOMLOE about the ¨participation, autonomy and ruling of schools¨ states that schools will have the autonomy to manage economic, material and human resources necessary to guarantee equal opportunities and quality education. Similarly, we find in the article 21.2 of the Royal Decree 157/2022 that the education administrations will be responsible for the contribution to the development of the curriculum by favouring the elaboration of open models of teaching programmes and teaching materials that meet the different needs of students and teachers, under the principles of the Universal Design for Learning (UDL).

Both, resources and materials are an important part of every teacher's planning since they provide the necessary tools for learners to actively practice and apply the language they are learning. Moreover, materials and resources can be customized or adapted to meet the specific needs of learners, such as their age, level of proficiency, learning style, and interests. Overall, materials and resources are crucial for facilitating active, meaningful engagement with the language, which is key to language acquisition.

Among the human resources that can be found in a Primary school community not all of them necessarily need to be teachers. We may find people such as the janitor or caretaker, the librarian, the physio specialist, psychologist, etc. However, the majority of people that are going to be involved in the teaching process of our students are going to be teachers. Some of these teachers can be the management or administration staff and the teaching staff, including teaching coordinators, tutors and specialists. It is worth to mention that the role of the language assistant will play an important part in the case of the FL classes, since s/he may bring native language and cultural experiences into the classroom.

Didactic resources and materials refer to the tools and aids that are used to support learning. However, they are often used interchangeably, but they have slightly different meanings.

- **Resources** refer to the broader range of tools and aids that are available to support learning. These can include things like textbooks, online resources, equipment, and technology. Resources can also include facilities, such as libraries, computers room and laboratories (language lab, science lab, etc.).

- **Materials**, on the other hand, refer more specifically to the items that are used directly in the teaching and learning process. These can include things like worksheets, handouts, activity sheets, and other items that are used to support the curriculum. Materials can also include things like audio and visual aids, such as videos, flashcards, photos, maps, etc., which are used to supplement instruction.

In summary, resources are the broader category which includes materials, people, and facilities. Whereas materials are the specific things that are used to support the curriculum and instruction in the classroom.

The right selection and use of resources and materials in the FL classroom can greatly enhance the learning experience for students and improve their chances of using the language with a communicative purpose. Obviously, and following the guidelines from the UDL, we will need to align these materials with the curriculum, the students' age and needs, etc.

INFORMATION & COMMUNICATION TECHNOLOGY (ICT)

The **article 111 bis** about the Information and communication technologies (ICTs) in the law on education **LOMLOE 3/2020** states in its section 4 that the education administrations and the management staff in schools will promote the use of **information and communication technologies** in the classroom as an appropriate and valuable didactic means to carry out teaching and learning tasks. Moreover, technology and digital competences are included among the key competences of the curriculum (STEM) stated in the **article 9** of the **Royal Decree 157/2022**, which promote digital literacy, problem solving and critical thinking, at the same time that innovation, creativity, collaboration and teamwork.

ICTs refer to the various **tools** and **resources** that can be used to support teaching and learning in education. These can include computers, tablets, smartphones, internet access, and a variety of software and apps. There are many ways in which information and communication technologies (ICTs) can be used in a FL classroom in Primary education. Some **examples** include:

o **To practice vocabulary and grammar**: There are many online games and apps that can be used to help students practice vocabulary and grammar in a fun and interactive way. Some examples of popular online games for children to practice English grammar and vocabulary include:

  - https://www.mes-english.com/

  - https://www.vocabularist.com/

  - https://www.englishcentral.com/

  - https://www.funbrain.com/

  - https://www.digitaldialects.com/

  - https://learnenglishkids.britishcouncil.org/

  - https://www.quill.org/

o **To practice the oral skills**: ICTs can be used to provide students with access to audio and video resources, such as recordings of native speakers and authentic materials like songs, podcasts and news broadcasts, which can help to improve listening and speaking skills. Students can also use some online resources and apps to practice their speaking skills with more specific resources such as ¨voxopop¨, ¨voice thread¨, ¨voki¨, or even recording themselves on a video using the language in tasks, projects or drama activities.

o **To collaborate while learning**: ICTs can be used to facilitate collaborative learning activities, such as online calls and meetings with other European schools (KA2-Erasmus+), shared documents to be worked at home and discuss in the classroom (flipped classroom), doing virtual classes such as Zoom, Google Meats or Microsoft Teams for students that must stay home isolating due to illness or prevention (ex. Covid).

o **To foster interactive learning**: Interactive whiteboards and tablets can be used to create interactive and multimedia-rich learning experiences, such as simulations, virtual reality (VR) and augmented reality (AR) experiences, and games that can help to increase engagement and retention of information.

- To evaluate the teaching and learning experience: Some tools can be used to collect and analyse data on student learning, which can help teachers to identify areas of need, track progress, and adjust instruction accordingly. Examples include Class Dojo, Idoceo, Nearpod, Kahoot, Quizlet, and Socrative. On the other hand, there are also some tools that can be used by the students to evaluate or self-reflect on their own learning such as the e-Language Portfolio, language learning journals, etc.

In any case, it is important to note that when using ICTs in a FL classroom, we must ensure that the technology is used in a safe and responsible way that supports and enhances the teaching and learning process taking into account the students' age and ability or skills. Overall, the integration of ICT and STEM competence in education helps to promote a range of essential 21st century skills that will be important for the future of our students' success in school and beyond.

SCHOOL PLANS, PROJECTS & PROGRAMMES

Following with the recommendations from the Chapter 2 of the Title 5 found in the law LOMLOE 3/2020 about the participation, autonomy and ruling of schools, we find that schools must incorporate within the elaboration and development of their documents (School Education Plan and Annual General Programme), some educative and innovative plans, projects or programmes as strategies and actions to cater to the characteristics and needs of the students and improve academic results and experiences.

COEXISTENCE PLAN

Coexistence is among the principles and aims of the Spanish Education System, since it implies mutual respect, tolerance, and understanding of diversity. The article 124 from the law LOMLOE states that schools must draw up a coexistence plan, which should be incorporated into the Annual General Programme, collecting all the norms, measures, and activities to promote coexistence and guarantee respect and equity to all the students and members of the school community.

This document is designed to promote a positive and safe learning environment for students and staff, at the same time that establishes a system for involving the whole school community, both students, parents, and teachers, in the development and implementation of the plan.

The coexistence plan is an important document for the school, and it is reviewed periodically to ensure that it is updated and effective. This plan should be shared with the school community at school or through the website, and all members of the school community are expected to follow it.

READING ENCOURAGMENT PLAN

Reading is a fundamental linguistic skill that enables individuals to acquire and process information, to learn, and to engage with the world around them. For this reason, reading is integrated among the principles and stage general objectives of the Primary Education (articles 16, 17 and 19, LOMLOE 3/2020).

The article 19 of the law LOMLOE states that reading comprehension, together with oral and written expression among other skills, must be worked in all areas of Primary Education. In its section 3, it also says that "a daily time will be devoted to reading" as well as the necessary implication of the administration and schools to promote and set plans for reading.

The Reading Encouragement Plan is a school document that outlines the strategies and activities that the school will implement to promote reading among students. The goal of the plan is to develop the students' reading skills and to foster a love of reading. The plan typically includes the following elements:

- Incorporating reading into the curriculum, such as through reading comprehension exercises and book reports. Setting reading goals for the students, such as increasing the number of books read or the number of minutes spent reading.

- Creating a reading-friendly environment in the classroom and the school library, with comfortable seating and a wide selection of books, and providing students with a diverse range of reading materials, such as books, magazines, newspapers, and digital resources.

- Organizing reading-related activities and events, such as book clubs, author visits, and reading competitions. Also, involving parents and the community in the reading promotion efforts, such as through reading programs and activities for families.

- Providing training and resources for teachers to help them integrate reading into their instruction.

This plan should be reviewed and updated regularly as well, to make sure that it continues to meet the needs of students and to ensure that the goal of the plan is met. The reading encouragement plan is an essential document for the school, and its implementation should involve the cooperation and collaboration of all members of the school community, including teachers, students, parents, and the community.

ERASMUS+ PROJECTS

In the article 103 of the law on education LOMLOE 3/2020 we find that the Ministry of Education is determined to promote international mobility of teachers through exchanges or educational visits to other countries, as a way of improvement, progress and training for teachers in public schools. Additionally, students may benefit from their teacher's experiences and training abroad.

On the other hand, students learning a FL may enjoy with the establishment of some connections with other European schools that use or learn a common language providing more opportunities to meet other people and learn and improve that language.

In this sense, Erasmus+ is a European Union (EU) programme that aims to support education, training, youth, and sport in Europe. It provides funding for a wide range of activities and projects to ensure international cooperation establishing school networks and partnership among schools and organizations from different countries.

In Primary Education it is a great way to give opportunities to access new teaching methods, resources, and professional development opportunities to improve the quality of education. It also provides students with opportunities to meet and work with other children from different countries through different projects (KA-2) contributing to the development of important social and emotional skills, such as teamwork, communication, and problem-solving.

Among the teacher duties established in the article 91 of the law LOMLOE 3/2020 we find the promotion, organization, and participation in complementary activities in and out of the school. Additionally, the article 88 of the same law states that these activities which are considered interesting and necessary for the development of the curriculum must be planned accordingly.

These complementary activities are those activities that supplement and enhance the learning experience from a traditional classroom setting. They may include field trips, guest speakers, hands-on projects, service learning from someone out of school, etc. The goal of these activities is to provide students with additional opportunities to develop skills and interests, and to make learning more engaging and relevant.

The complementary activities selected by the FL teachers, in our case, in coordination with the tutor teachers of the classes we teach English, will try to motivate and encourage the students to use the language, reinforce their FL linguistic skills, and ease their approach and knowledge of the English-speaking countries and their culture. These activities will be carefully planned in line with the FL curriculum. They must be reviewed along the year in case there is a need to change dates or any possible inconveniences that may arose. In general, these activities must be planned to contribute to the achievement of the intended goal in FL teaching, that is, the development of our students' communicative competence and cultural awareness of the foreign language.

Some examples of these activities may include:

o **In school** visits from a storyteller, theatre company, or native speakers to talk about a specific topic.

o **Out of the school** field trips to a nearby airport, touristic resort, theme park, the theatre, museums, etc.

As we can see, the variety of complementary activities that can be planned for the FL classes is very diverse. In any case, we must be aware that these activities should help to engage students in the learning process, making it more interactive and enjoyable, in order to increase their motivation to learn the language and help them see real-life contexts for language learning to understand the culture and the way the language is used in different settings.

In most cases, these complementary activities can be related in a multi or interdisciplinary way to other subjects in order to promote working some of the transversal elements of the curriculum. Therefore, some values related to non-discrimination, affection, safety, prevention of violence and sustainable development are usually worked among these activities. These complementary activities clearly contribute to the improvement and knowledge of the necessary skills to live in our current society, and therefore they are very much connected to the key competences of the curriculum.

Evaluation is a systematic process of collecting and analysing information from different sources to value the progress and performance of the students, as well as the impact and effectiveness of the teaching methods, resources and materials planned and used in our teaching practice.

Therefore, evaluation is an integral part of our teaching practice and must be coherent with all the elements involved in the curriculum. This evaluation has a clear guiding function which allows us to provide measures for modification regarding both the teaching and the learning process. The teacher will assess the level of achievement of the intended objectives for Primary Education applying the necessary methodology, bearing in mind the acquisition of the key competences through the evaluation criteria of the specific competences, and using different resources and instruments for the assessment.

According to the article 14 of the Royal Decree 157/22022, this evaluation will be global, continuous and formative, and will take into account the student's progress in the degree of development of the key competences in all areas.

TYPES OF EVALUATION

As we previously said, evaluation involves assessing not only the students' learning and progress but also the effectiveness of instructional methods, resources and materials. The results of educational evaluations are used to make **decisions** about curriculum planning, classroom arrangement, timing, and the selection of resources and material among others.

In order to carry out an appropriate evaluation of the whole teaching and learning practice, we may classify this concept of evaluation into some more specific **categories**:

- Diagnostic assessment: This type of evaluation is used to identify student's specific needs and to plan instruction accordingly. It is often used prior to planning the teaching programme and at the beginning of each unit of instruction to determine what students already know and what they need to learn. As established in the **article 22** from the **Royal Decree 157/2022**, there is also a diagnostic evaluation that must be conducted during the 4th year of Primary Education to check the progress of the student's development of the key competences (see also article 144.1 of LOMLOE 3/2020). The results of this evaluation shall be only of informative and orientative nature for the school, the students and their families.

- Continuous or formative assessment: This type of evaluation provides ongoing feedback on strengths and weaknesses to teachers and students during the instructional and learning process. As it is stated in the **section 2** from the **article 14** of the **Royal Decree 157/2022**, in the context of this continuous assessment process some education reinforcement measures must be established as soon as difficulties are detected.

- Summative assessment: This type of evaluation contributes to measure student learning and achievement of the intended goals and competences at the end of each unit or the school year. It is often used to determine the student's final grade in each subject at the end of the units or the whole academic year.

- **Global evaluation:** A broad, comprehensive assessment that looks at the overall effectiveness, efficiency, or impact of our teaching practice in relation not only to our area but also taking into account the rest of evaluation results from other area teachers. The student's exit profile, for example, is a combination of those results from different areas in relation to the development of the key competences by each student.

All these types of evaluation procedures are important for the contribution to the improvement of the education and teaching and learning practice.

EVALUATION PROCEDURES & INSTRUMENTS

As regarded in the article 14.5 from the Royal Decree 157/2022, the teaching staff will coordinate for the evaluation of the students' progress along the year and in a single evaluation session that should take place at the end of the school year. In its article 25 we may also find the different evaluation documents and reports for the official assessment of students in the Primary Education stage, namely the evaluation minutes, the academic transcript and records and the end-of-stage report among others.

According to the article 26 of this Royal Decree, the results from the evaluation shall be expressed in the following terms: "Insufficient (IN)", for negative marks, and "Sufficient (SU)", "Good (BI)", "Notable (NT)", and "Outstanding (SB)", for positive marks.

Almost every education administration of each Autonomous Community has developed some kind of technological evaluation tool to gather the information obtained through the evaluation of the students and keep track of their progress. This information can be shared with the school administration, other teachers in the same class and the student's family (evaluation report).

In our daily teaching practice, the reference for the assessment of the students' learning and progress shall be the evaluation criteria of the FL area curriculum, which are going to determine the degree of acquisition of the specific competences by our students since they are linked to them. These evaluation criteria are based on the descriptors of the Common European Framework of Reference for languages (CEFR) but adapted to the characteristics of the student at this age in Primary Education.

As stated in the article 14.6 of the RD 157/2022, varied, diverse and accessible evaluation instruments adapted to the different learning situations that allow for the objective assessment of all students shall be promoted. To this matter, we can say that either quantitative or qualitative ways of assessing students can be used to obtain a wider variety of information from their learning process.

Some examples of these tests could be:

EVALUATION INSTRUMENTS						
QUANTITATIVE		QUALITATIVE				
Oral test	Written test	Observation	Interview/Q&A	Records/Diary	Checklist	Rating scale

In most of the cases when using these instruments of evaluation we can use qualifications or marks that can be expressed in the form of numbers or any other type of scale in relation to some items or criteria selected to be assessed. However, in some other cases, as it is keeping notes on records or diaries, it is more difficult to score the students and we can only obtain some valuable information and feedback to reaffirm or ensure some of our previous records.

As we can see, the evaluation instruments are broad, and they can be split into different strategies that are going to be focused on specific activities and moments that can give us better information to assess our students. Some examples could be role plays, oral presentations, written dictations, worksheets, written exams, online resources (Kahoot!, Quizlet, Edpuzzle, Nearpod, Plickers, Seesaw, etc.),

Apart from these strategies, we can also count on peer and self-assessment as a way of reflection of the students own learning, contributing this way to lifelong learning and providing some feedback to other classmates on their learning and the teacher about the teaching practice, the resources and methods used. Some examples of these type of strategies could be:

- Feedback after project presentations or debates
- Cooperative work
- European Language Portfolio (paper or electronic version)
- Language Journal
- Gamification scoreboard
- Exit tickets
- Self-reflection target, chart or diagram.
- Etc.

In any case, the results and feedback obtained from the teacher's evaluation and the student's self-evaluation can provide very valuable information on the degree of implication and satisfaction with that intended plan that is our teaching programme. To this matter, teachers must also be constantly evaluating their own teaching practice and do some reflection on whether this plan is working.

EVALUATION OF THE TEACHING PRACTICE

The evaluation of the teaching practice has as its main goal the improvement of the quality in education through the assessment and self-reflection of the teaching experience. It is usually regulated by some legislative document of reference in each Autonomous Community providing some type of orientations and guidelines for its development. It can take place during a specific time devoted to this evaluation in the three terms or at the end of the school year.

The article 14 of the Royal Decree 157/2022, in its section 4, states that teachers shall assess both the students' learning and their own teaching practice. To this end, some aspects can be suggested to be observed and considered when carrying out this assessment:

❑ **Teacher coordination measures**, such as number of sessions attended for the coordination and evaluation of the students, etc.

❑ **Teaching programme adjustments**. For example, checking whether the time and number of sessions planned were appropriate, the curricular elements were properly sequenced and implemented, the resources used met the students' needs and interests, the evaluation procedures and instruments were in accordance with the situation, etc.

❑ **Satisfaction of the families and the students**. Checking the overall degree of satisfaction through personal interviews, tutoring sessions, parents' meetings, coordination, etc.

BIBLIOGRAPHY & REFERENCES

Lawful references:

- Organic **Law 3/2020**, December 29th, Modifying the Organic Law 2/2006 on Education.

- **Royal Decree 157/2022**, March 1st, establishing the National Curriculum of Primary Education.

- Council of Europe (2020) *Common European Framework of Reference for Languages: Leaning, Teaching, Assessment*. Companion Volume. Council of Europe Publishing, Strasburg.

- (ANY LEGAL DOCUMENT FROM YOUR <u>AUTONOMOUS COMMUNITY</u> CONCERNING CURRICULUM, ORGANIZATION & EVALUATION)

Authors:

- Antúnez et. Al. (2010) *Del proyecto educativo a la programación de aula*. Graó. Barcelona.

- Guillén Díaz, C.; Castro Prieto, P.(1998) *Manual de Autoformación para una Didáctica de la Lengua-cultura Extranjera*. Madrid, La Muralla.

- Piccardo, E., & North, M. (2019). *The Action-oriented Approach: A dynamic vision of language education*. Bristol, UK: Multilingual Matters.

- Piqueres Granero, M. (2022) *Programar en LOMLOE. Guía Paso a Paso*. 2ª Edición.

- Piqueres Granero, M. (2022) *Evaluar Competencias Clave y Sus Descriptores Operativos*. LOMLOE. 2ª Edición.

Websites:

- https://educagob.educacionyfp.gob.es/inicio.html

- https://intef.es/

- https://www.coe.int/en/web/common-european-framework-reference-languages

- http://www.teachingenglish.org.uk

- http://davidnunan.com/

LEARNING SITUATIONS
IN FL TEACHING

PART 1

In this document we will try to address all the essential aspects to understand what learning situations are and how to elaborate them for our FL lessons.

As we know, the **concept** of learning situations is described in the article 2 of the Royal Decree 157/2022 as ¨*situations and activities that involve the students' development of **actions** associated with **key competences** and **specific competences** that contribute to the acquisition and development of these competences*¨.

The Spanish Education System must adapt to the progress and changes in our society. Therefore, the new curricular development introduces and encourages a shift of focus from a content-based approach, where teachers mainly transmit certain knowledge that students must learn, to a competency-based approach, where students are active agents in their own learning process while developing the ability to solve problems, think critically and work collaboratively in teams, in order to face the challenges of the 21st century. These competences are regarded by the **Council of Europe** as essential skills for personal, social, and cognitive development of the students as well as for future success for their lifelong learning.

The achievement of these competences obviously requires a change of methodology that recognises the student as the agent of his/her own learning. For this reason, it is essential the implementation of pedagogical proposals that focus on the students' interests and allow them to construct knowledge with autonomy and creativity based on their own learning experiences.

Learning situations represent an effective way to integrate the curricular elements and basic knowledge from the different areas (interdisciplinarity) through meaningful and contextualised tasks and activities to solve problems in a group work. Which solution is transferable to other situations. Therefore, the teacher must **plan** and **design** learning situations with useful and functional **tasks** and **activities**, based on close and **familiar contexts** that are meaningful to the students, that present **challenges** that can be worked in a creative and cooperative way, and awaken their desire and curiosity to continue learning.

Therefore, it is **not only** about identifying or classifying healthy and unhealthy food and learn about the healthy eating plate, for example, **but** going beyond. Learning situations create a learning context that allows students to transfer what they learn in school to real life. For example, making a campaign to show pamphlets about the importance of healthy habits and responsible consumption (SDG#12) to make the school community (families and students) aware of the importance of healthy living. Another option could be working on a project about sustainable food in the future which are environmentally friendly, designing some possible solutions for reducing pollution, food waste and packaging.

These learning experiences should involve the use of different **resources** that promote the development of cognitive, emotional, and psychomotor processes in students. They should also favour different types of **grouping** (individual work, pair work, small groups, or large groups) and contribute to successful learning by encouraging **motivation**, differentiated instruction (**UDL**) dealing with students' **multiple intelligences** (Gardner), and scaffolding throughout the process in order to cater to diversity, and contributing to good classroom and school climate management and social cohesion. Finally, the **products** or **challenges** chosen must be suitable for the observation of the learning described in the **assessment criteria** in the curriculum. They also must be coherent with the personal, social, and cognitive development of the student.

If we focus on the recommendations of the **European Union** (Enriching 21st Century Language Education, Council of Europe, 2022), the Action-oriented Approach (AoA) is regarded as the new language learning paradigm that goes beyond the ¨Communicative Language Teaching¨ (CLT) or ¨Communicative Approach¨ and takes task-based learning to a higher level where the class and the outside world are integrated in genuine communicative practices. This approach is also known as action-based teaching (especially in America) and is very similar to the more developed version of the Task-based Language Teaching (TBLT) proposed by Van den Branden and his colleagues (2009). Therefore, this approach is associated with **'scenarios'** or **learning situations** for group tasks or projects that allow students initiative to solve real-life communicative needs.

Language use and language learning are both cognitive and social activities, therefore, students must be seen as 'social agents' who use languages to communicate in the real world, to create and mediate meaning, often in collaboration. Moreover, there is a swift of focus from what students 'know' about the language, to what the students **'can do'** with the language in different contexts. The learner/social agent thus mobilises all his/her resources (cognitive, emotional, linguistic, and cultural) and develops strategies, including the exploitation of accessible objects, tools, people and other funds of knowledge, in order to plan, to produce results and to monitor his/her action. The experience of monitoring the action further develops those competences and strategies (Council of Europe 2001) for lifelong learning.

Language education should therefore create learning contexts that encourage learners to grow in their role as social and collaborative agents, as autonomous and responsible language users/learners. Essentially, this means that the language curriculum should include **tasks** and/or **projects** that allow learners the space to take the initiative, collaborate, plan, and produce something. Learners as social agents can then take responsibility for their learning process, further developing their language repertoire (plurilingualism) as powerful lifelong learners.

Action orientation involves task/projects, usually in the form of 'scenarios' or learning situations that allow taking the initiative, so learners can purposefully and strategically exert their agency. Scenarios in which the learners have a defined mission to produce a proposal, artefact or other product under defined conditions and **constraints** (Bourguignon 2010) and which require co-construction of meaning through **mediation** and **interaction**. The way the CEFR Companion volume puts this is as follows:

> Above all, the action-oriented approach implies purposeful, collaborative tasks in the classroom, the primary focus of which is **not language**. If the primary focus of a task is not language, then there must be some other product or outcome (such as planning an outing, making a poster, creating a blog, designing a festival or choosing a candidate).

Action-oriented scenarios are usually developed through steps which involve the communicative activities of **reception**, **production**, **interaction** and the **mediation** of concepts and/or **communication**, inspired by CEFR descriptors (CEFR-CV, 2020) and developed in our National Curriculum. The final phase of the scenario is the collaborative production of an artefact or performance. Learners decide how to accomplish the task/project; teachers provide language input, resources, and support to class, group or individuals as required. There is a focus on autonomy and authenticity of materials, topics, and practices. Self-assessment and/or peer assessment of results with selected descriptors is quite common (find more information in "Enriching 21st Century Language Education, 2022, pages 30, 31 & 32).

But, how do we elaborate these scenarios or learning situations for our **FL class in Primary Education**? how do we know our students' interests and needs? what elements should we focus on? when do we introduce the activities that are going to help the students acquire certain abilities to solve the problem?

The elaboration of learning situations must be understood as dynamic and continuous, flexible and open, and must be adapted to the circumstances, needs and interests of the students.

Before working on the development of learning situations, we must be aware of the intentions of our plan. Therefore, the first step would be to have a clear idea of the **age** and academic **level** of the group of students to whom we are planning these situations. Also, we must have access to and analyse the curriculum for this specific level and know beforehand the specific competences, evaluation criteria, and basic knowledge of the different areas involved (Curriculum for your Autonomous Community).

Keeping in mind the age, interests and needs of the students, the curriculum provided as guidelines for our work, and the social demands we consider can be tackled to provide meaningful learning, then, we can start thinking about the possible learning situations or scenarios to be planned.

Obviously, having this previous information in mind, ideally, the second step would be to start considering possible titles that may be attractive and interesting to our students, and plan the appropriate timing that will be required to develop each one of these scenarios along the academic year. Then, we must follow the next steps or **sections** for the elaboration of each learning situation:

1. **Contextualization**
2. **Justification**
3. **Description of the task**
4. **Selection of the methodology**
5. **Curricular elements involved**
6. **Measures to cater to diversity**
7. **Evaluation**
8. **Sequencing of activities**

But let us examine one by one all of these elements to better understand how we can elaborate our learning situations in FLT.

1. CONTEXTUALIZATION

The first obvious thing to do when planning learning situations is to provide a short text with an explanation of the **context** where this situation is going to be implemented and developed. That is, give information about the school, the specific academic level implied, the age of these students and their specific characteristics, etc. Something that we should have thought about even before starting to develop a learning situation. Therefore, in this section we may focus on 2 different aspects:

- o In relation to the description of the school, we can make use of the school **Educational Project** to analyse its geographical situation, the school documents (plans and projects), ethos, its community and population, cultural and socio-economic background, surrounding facilities, resources, schedule, services, etc.

- o Concerning the group of students, we can make reference to their age (developmental stage), level (school year within the Primary Education stage), number of students, specific familiar context, students with specific education support needs (ACNEAE), areas of interest, basic knowledge already acquired, strengths and weaknesses, expectations, motivation, needs, etc.

Let's consider an example of a **group of 24 students in Year 5** from a school in an urban area with a mixture of low, mid, and high socioeconomic status. We will describe some more along the process.

2. JUSTIFICATION

The justification of the learning situation pretends to give light to the reasons why we are going to work that specific learning situation in our classroom. Therefore, we must focus on the analysis of situations that suit the needs and interests of the students. These situations can be aligned with real life problems and challenges of the 21st century, such as the ¨Sustainable Development Goals¨ (SDG), responsible use of Information and Communication Technologies (ICT), community service, problem solving, cooperative and collaborative work, communication and exchange of information, cultural manifestations, etc.

In the end, each learning situation must be related to some extent to the development of the key competences of the curriculum and will contribute to the teacher's collection of information on the degree of development of these competences expressed in the student's exit profile.

One example could be: ¨*The headteacher in the school has been informed that with time there are fewer and fewer students checking out books from the school library. We know how important reading is for exploring, enjoying, and learning from good books. We want to motivate the students in the school to visit the library more often. We thought maybe our class can do something to make the students aware of the benefits of using the library*¨.

The justification of a learning situation must be focused on intended tasks or projects to be worked collaboratively. However, we must not forget that it is essential that they are close to the students' experience, previous knowledge, and they must be relevant for their daily life. The focus must be put on the student as a social agent that is able to solve problems or produce something that is useful in present and even future situations.

Sometimes, the justification and the description of the intended task for the learning situation can be part of the same section (depending on personal interests and specification of the Autonomous Community for its elaboration). Therefore, we may justify the intended task and give a description of how it is going to be developed at the same time.

However, and considering the description as the definition of the challenge presented and the explanation of the intended outcome, we may do this in a separate section.

In this section, we can give **information** about what we expect from our students to do at an initial stage, during the task and as a final outcome for the specific learning situation. Therefore, with this description we try to respond to questions like:

WHAT? – What we want our students to learn during this process.

HOW? – How they can do to explore different options to give a solution.

WHY? – Why we want our students to learn something new.

Therefore, the description of the learning situation or scenario we are going to present to our students may be written following the next steps: *"The students will ... using ... in order to ..."*.

We must keep in mind the fact that the activities and the intended outcome of the task must be realistic, close to the students' interests, capacities and needs. Throughout the learning process involved in the development of the task, the students will be working on the development of some **key competences** that will be put together in the form of simple activities that will contribute to acquire some knowledge, skills, abilities, etc., which can also be transferable to other situations.

One example of a definition of a task could be: *"The students will work in groups to plan and develop an advertising campaign using different audio-visual resources in different formats to express clear and catchy messages that can be presented and displayed in the school, in order to make the whole school community aware of the importance of reading and using the library more frequently"*.

Of course, this section of the description of the task or challenge can be even more elaborated giving very clear examples of the process that is going to lead to the intended outcome in the task. We may focus on general aspects, as in this previous example, or give specific details on how big the groups are going to be, what resources are going to be used, what strategies are going to be followed, etc.

In the case of **FLT**, in an initial stage we must provide the learners with the necessary support and tools for language and content work to be used throughout the process. Thus, it is important to scaffold their learning providing the necessary information they may need to focus on the task. This can be done through activities with the whole class or in small groups that are going to contribute to work specific vocabulary, grammatical structures, pronunciation, etc., necessary to convey meaning in the communication process, that is, during the task and at the end with their outcome.

Ideally, and following the different levels of cognitive skills provided in the revised category of Bloom's Taxonomy, the activities and tasks must follow a progression that starts focusing on activities that require students using some 'low order thinking skills' (LOTS) and move towards the achievement of the intended goals while working on 'high order thinking skills' (HOTS).

Bloom's Revised Taxonomy defines six levels of learning, ranging from basic recall and comprehension to more complex skills such as analysis, synthesis, and evaluation. This taxonomy is widely used in education to design lessons and assess student learning outcomes.

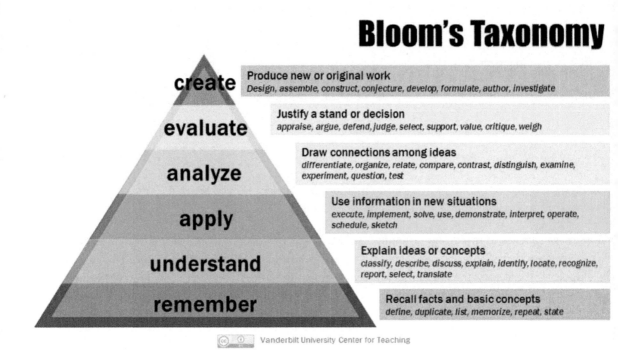

Considering these recommendations, we must plan activities that are going to be cognitively and psychologically appropriate for our students presented in an orderly manner. The intended outcome must bring a little challenge to the student, not too easy and not too hard, and it must provide opportunities for self-reflection and evaluation.

Some possible outcomes in a task may include:

- Digital: video, blog, web, wiki, WebQuest, programming, diagram, podcast, comic, presentation, questionnaire, survey, tutorial, radio, TV show, AR, VR, etc.

- Arts & Craft: collage, lapbook, poster, map, mural, costume, painting, model, graphs, etc.

- Oral: presentation, debate, role play, dramatization, storytelling, interview, etc.

- Written: letter, email, article, news, story, recipe, poem, summary, route, plan, etc.

- Hands-on: experiment, market, shop, prototype, model, game, etc.

Once we have a better idea of what we want our students to learn in a specific **learning situation** and we have thought about the outcome of the **task**, it is time to think about the methodology we consider appropriate to work during this teaching and learning process. Obviously, **every context** in every learning situation may imply a **different approach** to work and address the intended task.

When we talk about the context, we refer to the students' characteristics (age, proficiency level, interests and needs, etc.) and the purpose and intention of the learning situation per se. Therefore, we may consider the following aspects:

- Concerning the **students' characteristics**, we must think of a methodology that suits all of the students in the classroom and gives opportunities to learn by doing, in line with the principles of the Universal Design for Learning (UDL). A "flipped classroom" methodology, for example, may not be the best way to work with very young students or students who have no access to technology at home for any reason.

- In relation to the **learning situation**, we should bear in mind the characteristics of the tasks and activities to be worked and the time needed. Therefore, we must think about the possible resources and materials we may need (digital or analogical), strategies to be used (group configurations, scaffolding, gamification, etc.), implication of other school or community members, relationship with other areas, evaluation procedures, and of course, the outcome expected at the end of the learning situation.

In any case, the teacher's decision on the selection of the methodology to be used will depend on his/her implication with the students, and his/her knowledge and mastery of the techniques of such methodology.

The current teaching approach in education focuses on a **constructivist** learning theory that suggests that the student must be seen as a **social agent** responsible for his/her own learning. This learner-centred approach implies the use of active learning methodologies that contribute to the participation and collaboration of the students through teamwork in tasks and projects (also suggested in the Action-oriented Approach). These tasks and projects will bring opportunities to the students to put into practice the use of life skills and competences that can be applied in further situations.

Among the different proposals that we currently have for second language learning we may highlight:

- Content and Language Integrated Learning (**CLIL**): CLIL is an approach where the FL is used as the medium of instruction for teaching non-language subjects, such as Science, Maths, or Social Studies. This transversal approach for interdisciplinarity can provide students with the opportunity to learn content and language simultaneously, in a more authentic and meaningful context.

- Task-based Language Teaching (**TBLT**): This is an approach that emphasises the use of communicative tasks as the primary means of language instruction. Students engage in tasks that are relevant and meaningful to them, such as planning a trip or giving a presentation. This approach encourages students to use the target language in a real-life context, and to develop the skills they need to communicate effectively.

- **Project-Based Learning (PBL):** PBL is an approach where students work on a project that is relevant to their interests and the curriculum (multidisciplinary). Projects can be completed in small groups or even at school level, and can include activities such as research, writing, and presentation. PBL provides students with the opportunity to use the target language in a real-life context, and also encourages collaboration and problem-solving skills that can be connected sometimes to raise awareness of the Sustainable Development Goals (SDG) proposed by the United Nations.

- **Game-based Learning:** This approach uses games, puzzles, and interactive activities as a way to engage students and provide them with opportunities to practice the target language in a fun and dynamic way. Game-based learning can also be used to motivate students and make learning more enjoyable.

- **Blended Learning:** This approach combines online and offline resources and activities, such as interactive language-learning software, videos, and games, with traditional classroom instruction (as it is the case of "**flipped classroom**"). Blended learning can be great for differentiated instruction since it allows students to work at their own pace and to review material they have previously covered. It can also provide teachers with valuable insights into how their students are progressing and what areas need to be covered more in-depth.

These are a few examples of current practices in FL instruction in Primary Education, other modern methodologies that can be considered are **Gamification**, **Cooperative** Learning, **Problem Based** Learning, **Service-Learning** Projects, or Teaching Proficiency through Reading and Storytelling (**TPRS**), among others. The specific approach will depend on the school, the students, and the resources available, but the goal is always to create a positive, effective, and real language learning experience for students.

5. CURRICULAR ELEMENTS INVOLVED

The integration of the curricular elements for a "learning situation" requires spending some time looking, analysing, and selecting those elements from the official curriculum. In most cases, these elements are very similar to the ones established in the Royal Decree 157/2022. However, with the decentralisation of our education system, each **Autonomous Community** has the freedom and responsibility of devising their own **curriculum**, and we may find some changes or extended versions in relation to each individual academic level of the Primary Education stage, the specific competences of each area, or even more specifications of elements included in the basic knowledge (generally, discourse and syntactic contents).

In any case, the national curriculum states the curricular elements summarised in the following chart:

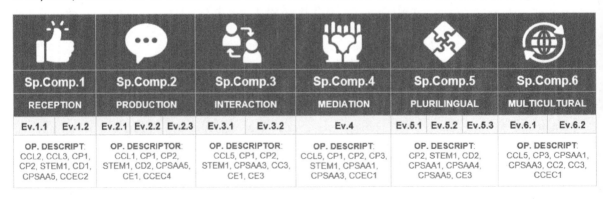

Sp.Comp.1		Sp.Comp.2			Sp.Comp.3		Sp.Comp.4	Sp.Comp.5			Sp.Comp.6	
RECEPTION		PRODUCTION			INTERACTION		MEDIATION	PLURILINGUAL			MULTICULTURAL	
Ev.1.1	Ev.1.2	Ev.2.1	Ev.2.2	Ev.2.3	Ev.3.1	Ev.3.2	Ev.4	Ev.5.1	Ev.5.2	Ev.5.3	Ev.6.1	Ev.6.2
OP. DESCRIPT: CCL2, CCL3, CP1, CP2, STEM1, CD1, CPSAA5, CCEC2		OP. DESCRIPTOR: CCL1, CP1, CP2, STEM1, CD2, CPSAA5, CE1, CCEC4			OP. DESCRIPTOR: CCL5, CP1, CP2, STEM1, CPSAA3, CC3, CE1, CE3		OP. DESCRIPT: CCL5, CP1, CP2, CP3, STEM1, CPSAA1, CPSAA3, CCEC1	OP. DESCRIPT: CP2, STEM1, CD2, CPSAA1, CPSAA4, CPSAA5, CE3			OP. DESCRIPT: CCL5, CP3, CPSAA1, CPSAA3, CC2, CC3, CCEC1	

When we are planning our units and learning situations for a specific group of students, we can start thinking first on the final goal we want to achieve, or we may want to see first these references from the curriculum to select the goals and activities. Therefore, we may consider these **2 options**:

1. **Top-down analysis**: Going from the established curriculum guidelines, and after careful reading and selection of those elements that we want to work in an orderly manner, that is, sequencing those curricular elements in time according to difficulty. Then, we can think of the possible units and learning situations that we can select to work those elements. We continue with the establishment of the goals, and we finish with the activities and tasks for our lessons.

2. **Bottom-up analysis**: We may prefer to decide first some possible tasks and activities we want to do in each unit or learning situation, and then, once we have developed a draft of ideas of each scenario with their intended goals, we select those curricular elements that are going to be worked in each one of those units.

Whatever option we decide to follow for the elaboration of our units and learning situations, it is advisable to keep in mind a holistic view of our planning and follow a logical progression of activities based on the evolution of students' learning process according to **Bloom's Taxonomy**, moving from low to high order thinking skills (LOTS & HOTS). That is, we should think first on those activities that are going to engage the student in learning making some connections (remember), provide some new input (understand) which need to be put into practice (apply), then, give them plenty of opportunities to manipulate new content and language (analyse), using cooperative work for self-reflection (evaluate) and reach to the elaboration of an outcome (create) that can be shared with the rest of the class and school community.

The curricular elements involved in each unit can be expressed in a table using the exact same statements from the official document, or they can be tweaked to reduce the number of words (always keeping the same meaning) saving some space in the document and being more precise on what is been conveyed.

An **example** of this table with those curricular elements could be:

YEAR	5	UNIT		9. Our school community	
Learning Situation	Open a book and open your mind!		**TIMING**	3rd Term – **5 lessons** Apr. 8th – Apr. 19th	
Justification	The headteacher in the school has been informed that with time there are fewer and fewer students checking out books from the school library. We know how important reading is for exploring, enjoying, and learning from good books. We want to motivate the students in the school to visit the library more often. We thought maybe our class can do something to make the students aware of the benefits of using the library.				
Description & Final task	The students will work in groups to plan and develop an advertising campaign using different audio-visual resources in different formats to express clear and catchy messages that can be presented and displayed in the school, in order to make the whole school community aware of the importance of reading and using the library more frequently.				
Primary Stage Objectives			FL Basic knowledge		
a) To know and appreciate the **values** and rules of **coexistence**, as well as the pluralism inherent in a democratic society. b) To develop habits of individual and **teamwork**, effort, and responsibility in their			A. COMMUNICATION - Self-confidence and reflection on learning. Error as an integral part of the process. - Basic strategies for comprehension, planning and production of texts.		

study, as well as attitudes of self-confidence, critical thinking, personal initiative, curiosity, interest, and creativity in learning, and entrepreneurial spirit.
e) To know and use appropriately the Spanish language and, if any, the co-official language of the Autonomous Community, and to develop **reading habits**.
f) To acquire in at least one **foreign language** the basic communicative competence that will enable them to express and understand simple messages and to cope in everyday situations.
j) Use different artistic **representations** and expressions and initiate in the construction of visual and audiovisual proposals.

Specific objectives

1. Increase students' motivation to read.
2. Foster a love for reading in the whole school community.
3. Use different means of representation for communication and expression of an idea.
4. Broaden cultural horizons through texts and foster lifelong love for reading.

- Knowledge, skills, and attitudes for mediation.
- Basic communicative functions: expressing ideas, persuading, giving directions, etc.
- Basic discourse genres (conversation, narrative, advertisements, etc.)
- Basic linguistic structures (Wh-questions, exclamation, etc.)
- Basic vocabulary of interest to students (books and library).
- Simple sound, accentual and intonation patterns.
- Simple spelling conventions and meaning associated with graphic elements (Fonts, etc.).
- Basic analogue and digital tools for oral, written and multimodal communication (posters, videos, etc.)

B. PLURILINGUALISM

- Strategies to compensate communication deficits (connections to own experience and knowledge).
- Strategies and tools for self-assessment and co-evaluation.

C. INTERCULTURALITY

- Basic sociocultural and sociolinguistic aspects (found in FL written books).
- Strategies to understand and appreciate linguistic, cultural and artistic diversity.

FL Specific competences	Competence O.D.	Evaluation criteria
1. RECEPTION	CCL2 CCL3 CP2 CD1	1.1 Recognise and understand words and expressions in short, simple oral, written, and multimodal texts. 1.2. Select, organise and apply strategies to understand and process information in different texts.
2. PRODUCTION	CCL1 CD2 CPSAA5 CCEC4	2.1. Express orally short and simple texts, previously prepared, using verbal and non-verbal resources. 2.2. Organise and write short, simple texts, previously prepared, using analogue and digital tools.
3. INTERACTION	CP1 CPSAA3	3.1. Plan and participate in short, simple interactive situations using a variety of resources.
4. MEDIATION	CP2 CP3 CPSAA1 CPSAA3 CCEC1	4.1. Identify and explain texts in situations in which diversity is considered, showing respect and empathy. 4.2. Select and apply strategies which help to build bridges and facilitate communication using physical or digital resources.
5. PLURILINGUALISM	CP2 CPSAA4 CPSAA5 CE3	5.1. Compare and contrast similarities and differences between languages, reflecting on use. 5.2 Use with autonomy strategies to improve their ability to communicate and learn the FL.
6. MULTICULTURALITY	CCL5 CPSAA3 CC2	6.3. Select and apply basic strategies to understand and appreciate linguistic, cultural and artistic diversity.

Link with other areas	SDG	UDL	Cognitive Styles
Spanish Language & Lit. Arts & Crafts	Goal 4: Quality Education Goal 5: Gender equality in texts	Engage: Motivation act. Represent: Resources Express: Final product	LOTS: Explain & share ideas HOTS: Create & present

As we can see, the identification and selection of curricular elements in a first instance, may or may not give us clear expectations of what activities we should plan for the development of a specific unit. However, they may guide us in the type of linguistic strategies, communicative function, grammatical structure, vocabulary, pronunciation, etc. as those elements that we may consider when planning the lessons. In any case, it may seem easier to start thinking first on the activities to reach the intended outcome of the task and leave the selection of the curricular elements for later.

One important thing to keep in mind when planning our units and learning situations is the consideration of the attention to diversity we may find in the class, since not all our students are going to present the same proficiency level in the foreign language. Therefore, a specific section must be devoted to this matter.

6. MEASURES TO CATER TO DIVERSITY

The laws LOE 2/2006 and LOMLOE 3/2020 promote equity in education and attention to diversity. Emphasis is placed on individualizing attention and recognizing the unique characteristics and needs of each student to promote inclusion and quality education. This includes early detection and prevention of learning difficulties and support mechanisms. The goal is to allow each student to reach their full potential based on their strengths, aptitudes, and preferences.

The FL teacher is responsible for guiding the educational process and coordinating with other teachers, specialists, and families. The law LOMLOE 3/2020 requires flexible teaching methods and assessments for students with special educational needs. Reinforcement mechanisms, including individual support and curricular adaptations, should be applied as soon as learning difficulties are detected. These measures must be included in the Attention to Diversity Plan and integrated into the educational project. The aim is to provide individualized attention and ensure that all students can achieve the intended goals, through modifications or adaptations of content or methods and extension activities for fast-finisher students. These issues should be constantly addressed following the Universal Design for Learning guidelines.

UNIVERSAL DESIGN FOR LEARNING

Universal Design for Learning (UDL) is an educational framework that aims to make learning accessible to all students, including those with disabilities. It is based on three principles: multiple means of **representation, expression**, and **engagement**. These principles provide students with different ways to access, engage with, and express their understanding of the material. UDL seeks to reduce barriers and increase opportunities for learning by offering a wide range of options for students to learn, demonstrate their learning, and participate in the learning process, taking into account the various **learning styles** and **multiple intelligences** of students.

Examples of UDL strategies for FL teaching and learning include:

a. **REPRESENTATION**: using multiple media to present concepts, vocabulary, grammar, etc.

b. **EXPRESSION**: offering different ways for students to demonstrate their understanding, such as through drawing, writing, oral presentations, tasks, projects, etc.

c. **ENGAGEMENT**: creating interactive activities to engage students and allow them to practice the language.

UDL should be applied appropriately to meet the needs of specific students and should promote active learning methodologies such as task-based learning and content-based instruction. It helps remove barriers and increase opportunities for learning.

STUDENTS WITH SPECIFIC EDUCATIONAL SUPPORT NEEDS

Students with specific educational support needs (ACNEAE), are those who require additional support to access and engage in the curriculum. The article 71 of the law LOMLOE 3/2020 refers to these students as those ¨*who require educational attention different from the rest due to special education needs, developmental delay, language and communication development disorders, attention (ADHD) or learning disorders, severe lack of knowledge of the language of learning, or socio-educational vulnerability.*¨

The education administration in each Autonomous Community provides guidelines for the attention to students with specific educational support needs, but the classification of these students may vary based on regional laws and education policies.

The title 2 of the law on education (LOE 2/2006 and LOMLOE 3/2020) devoted to equity in education provides a different classification from previous years. Nevertheless, it still keeps the three main sections that establish the following **categories**:

1. Students with special education needs (SEN): The **article 73** of the law **LOMLOE 3/2020** defines the students with special education needs as those who face barriers that limit their access, presence, and participation in learning due to disabilities or serious behavioural, communication, and language disorders, and who require specific supports and educational attention to achieve the learning objectives. Examples of students with special education needs are students with intellectual disabilities, physical disabilities, sensory impairment, severe behaviour, communication, and language disorders, and multiple disabilities.

2. High ability students **or** gifted and talented students: High ability students are those who have demonstrated exceptional abilities in academics, music, arts, or other areas. These students may require specialized instruction or enrichment activities to challenge them and help them reach their full potential. However, in primary education, more specific measures and diagnoses are not generally conducted until the 3rd level of the stage.

3. Late entry students into the Spanish Education System: Late entry students are those who enter the Spanish education system later than the typical age at which students begin their studies. This can happen for a variety of reasons such as immigration, family circumstances, or delays in the educational

system. These students may face additional challenges such as language barriers or gaps in their knowledge, but there are programs and resources available to help them succeed.

4. **Students with specific learning difficulties**: Under this category, we may find several groups of students with learning difficulties such as dyslexia, dysgraphia, dyscalculia, ADHD, language specific disorder, non-verbal disorder, etc. There are also other learning difficulties that are not grouped or categorised, but still require support in schools when they face any barrier in their learning process.

In conclusion, students with specific educational support needs have different needs and the support that works for one student may not work for another. In a student-centred approach, where the needs of each individual student are considered and a variety of strategies and resources are used to support the student, it is essential to consider these differences to provide the necessary support. It is recommended to read the legislative reference documents that regulate the attention to diversity in your Autonomous Community.

If we take our previous example of a class in year 5, we may find a wide variety of students with their own individual differences, and we should explicitly say what are the characteristics of this particular group. Therefore, we must understand those individual needs and plan lessons and activities that are flexible and can be adjusted to meet the unique learning needs and abilities of each student, as the UDL suggests.

This may involve putting in place some general measures such as differentiated or individualized instruction, flexible grouping (pairs or small group, whole class work, etc. allowing teachers to group students according to their learning needs and abilities), graded tasks and activities, etc.

On the other hand, in the case of students with specific educational support needs who require some additional help, we could make use of some specific measures to accommodate or modify the content and resources used during our lessons. This will depend on the unique learning needs of our students, but among those measures we could say individual tutoring and support, collaboration with specialists, parent involvement, flexible grouping to support less able students, adapting texts (both oral and written), providing support tools (lenses or magnifying glasses, technological devices, Braille, etc.), using visual support (gestures, pictures, etc.), positive behaviour support, etc.

To sum up, the goal of differentiated instruction is to help all students learn and succeed, regardless of their individual abilities and learning styles. By adapting our teaching methods, we can provide a more inclusive and effective learning environment for all students.

7. EVALUATION

Evaluation is a crucial part of teaching practice, serving as a tool for measuring the performance and progress of students, as well as the effectiveness of teaching methods and resources. The evaluation process involves collecting and analysing information from various sources and must be consistent with all elements of the curriculum. Teachers will assess the achievement of objectives for Primary Education through the use of various assessment methods and resources, with a focus on key competences.

According to the article 14 of the Royal Decree 157/22022, this evaluation will be global, continuous and formative, and will take into account the student's progress in the degree of development of the key competences in all areas.

TYPES OF EVALUATION

Evaluation involves assessing both the students' progress and the effectiveness of teaching methods, resources, and materials. The results of these evaluations are used to make decisions about the curriculum and other aspects of teaching. The different types of evaluations include:

- □ diagnostic assessments, which identify student needs and plan instruction.

- □ continuous or formative assessments, which provide ongoing feedback during the instructional process.

- □ summative assessments, which measure student learning and achievement at the end of a unit or academic year.

- □ global evaluation, which focuses on the evaluation of the overall effectiveness of the teaching practice.

All these evaluations contribute to the improvement of education and the teaching and learning process.

TECHNIQUES & INSTRUMENTS

In our daily teaching practice, the reference for the assessment of the students' learning and progress shall be the evaluation criteria of the FL area curriculum, which are going to determine the degree of acquisition of the specific competences by our students since they are linked to them. These evaluation criteria are based on the descriptors of the Common European Framework of Reference for languages (CEFR) but adapted to the characteristics of the student at this age in Primary Education.

As stated in the article 14.6 of the RD 157/2022, varied, diverse and accessible evaluation instruments adapted to the different learning situations that allow for the objective assessment of all students shall be promoted. To this matter, we can say that either quantitative or qualitative ways of assessing students can be used to obtain a wider variety of information from their learning process and consider some possible ways for improvement, as we can see in the following examples:

EVALUATION INSTRUMENTS						
QUANTITATIVE		QUALITATIVE				
Oral test	Written test	Observation	Interview/Q&A	Records/Diary	Checklist	Rating scale

The results and feedback obtained from the teacher's evaluation and the student's self-evaluation provide valuable information on the degree of student involvement and development of the competences of the curriculum, as well as the success of our teaching programme.

Apart from these strategies, we can also count on peer and self-assessment as a way of reflection of the students own learning, contributing this way to lifelong learning and providing some feedback to other classmates on their learning and the teacher about the teaching practice, the resources and methods used.

In any case, the results and feedback obtained from the teacher's evaluation and the student's self-evaluation can provide very valuable information on the degree of implication and satisfaction with that intended plan that is our teaching programme. To this matter, teachers must also be constantly evaluating their own teaching practice and do some reflection on whether this plan is working.

8. SEQUENCING OF ACTIVITIES

Sequencing activities and tasks for FL learning is the process of arranging and organizing language activities in a logical and meaningful order. This may involve starting with simple activities that provide opportunities for students to practice using language in context, followed by more complex activities that challenge them to apply their language skills to more advanced tasks and problem-solving situations.

Following Bloom's Taxonomy as the natural process of cognitive development, the lower levels stages, such as recalling information and understanding concepts, can be the starting point for language learning activities. As learners progress, they can engage in more complex tasks, such as analysing, evaluating and creating, which can help to deepen their understanding of the language and its use.

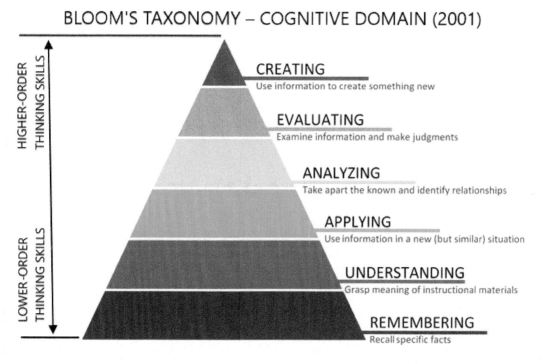

BLOOM'S TAXONOMY – COGNITIVE DOMAIN (2001)

HIGHER-ORDER THINKING SKILLS

LOWER-ORDER THINKING SKILLS

CREATING
Use information to create something new

EVALUATING
Examine information and make judgments

ANALYZING
Take apart the known and identify relationships

APPLYING
Use information in a new (but similar) situation

UNDERSTANDING
Grasp meaning of instructional materials

REMEMBERING
Recall specific facts

The Action-oriented Approach emphasizes the importance of hands-on, practical learning experiences in which learners actively use the language, rather than simply passively receiving information. This approach is well-aligned with **Bloom's Taxonomy** as it promotes as systematic progression towards the development of higher-level thinking skills (HOTS) and encourages learners to apply their knowledge and skills in real-life situations.

Therefore, in order to provide opportunities for students to understand and use the language in meaningful and practical ways, we may suggest the following sequence of activities to support an engaging learning environment and maximise student success:

INITIAL ACTIVITIES: Starting with initial activities, such as **checking previous knowledge**, helps to assess the students' prior knowledge and understanding of the subject, which is essential for effective teaching. These activities are related to the lower levels of Bloom's Taxonomy, such as **remembering** and **understanding**, and they allow the teacher to lay the foundation for the learning that will take place later in the sequence and ensure that students have the necessary background knowledge to be successful in the activities that follow. Some examples could be:

a. Brainstorming to determine what students already know about the topic.

b. Using graphic organisers to show or recall previous knowledge.

c. Reviewing and identifying key terms and concepts related to the topic.

MOTIVATION & DEVELOPMENT ACTIVITIES: They are aligned with certain levels of Bloom's Taxonomy concerning **understanding** and **applying**. These activities encourage students to engage with the material at a deeper level, apply their understanding in new and creative ways, and develop the skills and competencies they need to be successful. By making the subject matter interesting and relevant to the students, they are more likely to be invested in their own learning and be willing to work hard to achieve their goals. Some examples are:

a. Engaging hands-on activities to provide students with a concrete understanding of the topic.

b. Group work to foster collaboration and teamwork.

c. Interactive work or multimedia presentations to introduce the topic and stimulate critical thinking.

DESIGN ACTIVITIES: These activities imply more creative stages of Bloom's Taxonomy, since students must **apply** their knowledge, **analysing** and **evaluating** their progress in the design of tasks related to real-world problems and situations. In this phase, students may receive some kind of scaffolding and feedback about their progress. Some examples could be:

a. Individual or group planning activities to design a project, create a plan, or develop a proposal.

b. Mind-mapping activities to generate ideas and organize information for presentations.

c. Role-playing or scenario-based activities to explore different perspectives and challenges related to the topic.

APPLICATION ACTIVITIES: They refer to the levels between ¨**apply**¨ and ¨**create**¨ of Bloom's Taxonomy and allow students to demonstrate their understanding of the material in a more concrete, tangible way. In this phase students will end up with their final task, their outcome, after getting the necessary support along the process. Some examples are:

a. Opportunities for students to apply their knowledge and skills through real-world projects or simulations. For example, solving problems or carrying out experiments.

b. Observing and applying their knowledge following specific patterns or models.

c. Presenting final outcomes to be shared with classmates or the school community.

EVALUATION ACTIVITIES: These activities allow teachers and students to **evaluate** the effectiveness of the teaching method, resources, skills, procedures, etc. Some examples are:

b. Peer review or feedback sessions to help students reflect on their own work and improve their skills. For example: thumbs up!, exit tickets, checklists, etc.

c. Formative assessments, such as quizzes, tests, or homework assignments, to measure understanding and progress, etc.

d. Self-reflection through note taking, charts, checklists, targets, portfolios, language journals, diaries, etc.

These are just some examples and activities, but obviously they may vary depending on each specific topic and learning goals. An important aspect is to ensure a balance between all of the activities in order to create a supportive and engaging learning environment leading to the development of the key competences in the curriculum. For that reason, following a sequence of activities that go from low order thinking skills (LOTS) to high order thinking skills (HOTS) seems to be the best option.

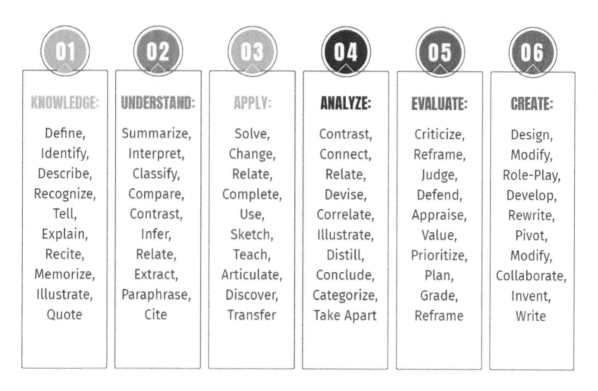

01 KNOWLEDGE:	02 UNDERSTAND:	03 APPLY:	04 ANALYZE:	05 EVALUATE:	06 CREATE:
Define, Identify, Describe, Recognize, Tell, Explain, Recite, Memorize, Illustrate, Quote	Summarize, Interpret, Classify, Compare, Contrast, Infer, Relate, Extract, Paraphrase, Cite	Solve, Change, Relate, Complete, Use, Sketch, Teach, Articulate, Discover, Transfer	Contrast, Connect, Relate, Devise, Correlate, Illustrate, Distill, Conclude, Categorize, Take Apart	Criticize, Reframe, Judge, Defend, Appraise, Value, Prioritize, Plan, Grade, Reframe	Design, Modify, Role-Play, Develop, Rewrite, Pivot, Modify, Collaborate, Invent, Write

Source: www.teachthought.com

Some teachers may prefer to synthesise all of these activities in only **3 types**: engagement, development and evaluation. In this case, engagement would be related to the first 2 stages of **Bloom's Taxonomy**. Development would be moving from the second to the next 2. And finally, evaluation activities would be at the last 2 stages, where students would check whether their outcome matches the intended goal of the task, and they draw some conclusions with their final creation.

1. **Engagement activities** would be those related to the initial and motivation stage at the beginning of a lesson. These activities must be designed to actively involve students in their FL learning process. They should create a pleasant learning environment, motivation and interaction.

2. **Development activities** would include all of the work the students must do to develop the task, starting from comprehension activities, practice, development of a specific outcome individually, in pairs or groups. Collaboration is going to be an essential factor for language development.

3. Finally, **evaluation activities** would be those where the children present their outcome to the teacher and classmates so that it can be assessed by the teacher and by the students themselves. Feedback and other instruments for the evaluation, both for the teacher and the students, would be necessary to keep track of the FL learning process and development of the key competences.

Different **group dynamics** must be planned to provide opportunities for communication and interaction. Therefore, the **space** distribution and classroom management will play an important part to provide this positive ambience for learning. Teachers must know very well the group of students to bring the best opportunities for learning. Some strategies we can use are mixing students in heterogeneous groups to help less able students or those with language proficiency difficulties, arranging some tables or corners (or learning stations) to gather and work in groups, allowing the **time** they need to develop the activities, task or project, etc. This time may be fixed or variable, depending on the situation. In most cases, the teacher must plan the timing of each activity developed in the classroom, but we must always keep in mind some factors that may vary that established plan. For example: class delay for any reason, time for further explanation in previous activities, technological problems, etc.

It seems obvious as well that the **resources** needed for each situation may vary, as they will be selected and used to cater to individual needs and characteristics of our students. Moreover, materials and resources must be customized or adapted to meet the specific needs of learners, such as their age, level of language proficiency, learning style, and interests. Overall, materials and resources are crucial for facilitating active, meaningful engagement with the language, which is key to language acquisition.

In the second part of this document, we will provide some examples of these activities in a complete lesson plan sequenced for a learning situation.

TEACHING PROGRAMME
FIRST IDEAS

WRITE ABOUT THE CONTEXT IN WHICH YOUR TEACHING PROGRAMME IS GOING TO BE BASED.

SCHOOL CONTEXT:

LOCATION: (District/Region, City, town, rural, neighbourhood, etc.)

LOCATION FEATURES:

SCHOOL FEATURES:

NUMBER OF STUDENTS/TEACHERS:

ETHNICITY:

FACILITIES:

TIMETABLE:

CLASS CONTEXT:

TEACHERS ATTENDING THE CLASS:

NUMBER OF STUDENTS:

CLASS FEATURES (AGE, INTERESTS, NEEDS, ...):

DIVERSITY (WHOLE CLASS):

ACNEAE (SPECIFIC INDIVIDUAL FEATURES):

Opospills

TEACHING PROGRAMME

FIRST IDEAS

ONCE YOU KNOW THE CLASS AND CONTEXT AND HAVE READ THE CURRICULUM IN DEPTH:

SELECT THE METHODOLOGY YOU ARE GOING TO FOLLOW

METHODOLOGY	
MAIN STRATEGIES	
RESOURCES	

NAME YOUR UNITS

YOU CAN COMPLETE THIS PART AT THE END
OR START WITH A DRAFT TO KNOW THE NUMBER OF LESSONS PER UNIT

TITLE	TIMING	SESSIONS

Opospills

UNIT 1 MAIN TOPIC (ex. Welcome back!):

APPROX LESSONS REQUIRED:

DOES IT NEED MORE THAN 1 LEARNING SITUATION? YES / NO

LEARNING SITUATION:

JUSTIFICATION:

DESCRIPTION (INCLUDE THE FINAL TASK):

UNIT 2 MAIN TOPIC (ex. On my way to school):

APPROX LESSONS REQUIRED:

DOES IT NEED MORE THAN 1 LEARNING SITUATION? YES / NO

LEARNING SITUATION:

JUSTIFICATION:

DESCRIPTION (INCLUDE THE FINAL TASK):

UNIT 3 MAIN TOPIC (ex. What's for dinner?):

APPROX LESSONS REQUIRED:

DOES IT NEED MORE THAN 1 LEARNING SITUATION? YES / NO

LEARNING SITUATION:

JUSTIFICATION:

DESCRIPTION (INCLUDE THE FINAL TASK):

UNIT 4 MAIN TOPIC (ex. Spooky story!):

APPROX LESSONS REQUIRED:

DOES IT NEED MORE THAN 1 LEARNING SITUATION? YES / NO

LEARNING SITUATION:

JUSTIFICATION:

DESCRIPTION (INCLUDE THE FINAL TASK):

UNIT 5 MAIN TOPIC:

APPROX LESSONS REQUIRED:

DOES IT NEED MORE THAN 1 LEARNING SITUATION? YES / NO

LEARNING SITUATION:

JUSTIFICATION:

DESCRIPTION (INCLUDE THE FINAL TASK):

UNIT 6 MAIN TOPIC:

APPROX LESSONS REQUIRED:

DOES IT NEED MORE THAN 1 LEARNING SITUATION? YES / NO

LEARNING SITUATION:

JUSTIFICATION:

DESCRIPTION (INCLUDE THE FINAL TASK):

UNIT 7 MAIN TOPIC:

APPROX LESSONS REQUIRED:

DOES IT NEED MORE THAN 1 LEARNING SITUATION? YES / NO

LEARNING SITUATION:

JUSTIFICATION:

DESCRIPTION (INCLUDE THE FINAL TASK):

UNIT 8 MAIN TOPIC:

APPROX LESSONS REQUIRED:

DOES IT NEED MORE THAN 1 LEARNING SITUATION? YES / NO

LEARNING SITUATION:

JUSTIFICATION:

DESCRIPTION (INCLUDE THE FINAL TASK):

UNIT 9 MAIN TOPIC:

APPROX LESSONS REQUIRED:

DOES IT NEED MORE THAN 1 LEARNING SITUATION? YES / NO

LEARNING SITUATION:

JUSTIFICATION:

DESCRIPTION (INCLUDE THE FINAL TASK):

UNIT 10 MAIN TOPIC:

APPROX LESSONS REQUIRED:

DOES IT NEED MORE THAN 1 LEARNING SITUATION? YES / NO

LEARNING SITUATION:

JUSTIFICATION:

DESCRIPTION (INCLUDE THE FINAL TASK):

UNIT 11 MAIN TOPIC:

APPROX LESSONS REQUIRED:

DOES IT NEED MORE THAN 1 LEARNING SITUATION? YES / NO

LEARNING SITUATION:

JUSTIFICATION:

DESCRIPTION (INCLUDE THE FINAL TASK):

UNIT 12 MAIN TOPIC:

APPROX LESSONS REQUIRED:

DOES IT NEED MORE THAN 1 LEARNING SITUATION? YES / NO

LEARNING SITUATION:

JUSTIFICATION:

DESCRIPTION (INCLUDE THE FINAL TASK):

Opospills

(IF YOUR AUTONOMOUS COMMUNITY REQUIRES MORE THAN 12 UNITS)

UNIT 13 MAIN TOPIC:

APPROX LESSONS REQUIRED:

DOES IT NEED MORE THAN 1 LEARNING SITUATION? YES / NO

LEARNING SITUATION:

JUSTIFICATION:

DESCRIPTION (INCLUDE THE FINAL TASK):

UNIT 14 MAIN TOPIC:

APPROX LESSONS REQUIRED:

DOES IT NEED MORE THAN 1 LEARNING SITUATION? YES / NO

LEARNING SITUATION:

JUSTIFICATION:

DESCRIPTION (INCLUDE THE FINAL TASK):

UNIT 15 MAIN TOPIC:

APPROX LESSONS REQUIRED:

DOES IT NEED MORE THAN 1 LEARNING SITUATION? YES / NO

LEARNING SITUATION:

JUSTIFICATION:

DESCRIPTION (INCLUDE THE FINAL TASK):

Use this template to draft the lessons for each unit. Copy and paste as needed:

UNIT 1:	LESSONS
	LESSON 1:
RESOURCES: (Weblinks of books, videos, songs, games, etc.)	LESSON 2:
	LESSON 3:
DUA: Engagement: Motivation activities Representation: Resources Expression: Final product	LESSON 4:
Cognitive skills: LOTS: HOTS:	LESSON 5:
	LESSON 6:
SDG: Goal 4. Quality education	(Add as needed)
EVALUATION: Formative (continuous) Summative (final)	

Cognitive skills chart:

01 KNOWLEDGE:	02 UNDERSTAND:	03 APPLY:	04 ANALYZE:	05 EVALUATE:	06 CREATE:
Define, Identify, Describe, Recognize, Tell, Explain, Recite, Memorize, Illustrate, Quote	Summarize, Interpret, Classify, Compare, Contrast, Infer, Relate, Extract, Paraphrase, Cite	Solve, Change, Relate, Complete, Use, Sketch, Teach, Articulate, Discover, Transfer	Contrast, Connect, Relate, Devise, Correlate, Illustrate, Distill, Conclude, Categorize, Take Apart	Criticize, Reframe, Judge, Defend, Appraise, Value, Prioritize, Plan, Grade, Reframe	Design, Modify, Role-Play, Develop, Rewrite, Pivot, Modify, Collaborate, Invent, Write

Opospills

UNIT 2:	LESSONS
	LESSON 1:
RESOURCES: (Weblinks of books, videos, songs, games, etc.)	LESSON 2:
	LESSON 3:
DUA: Engagement: Motivation activities Representation: Resources Expression: Final product	LESSON 4:
Cognitive skills: LOTS: HOTS:	LESSON 5:

01 KNOWLEDGE:	02 UNDERSTAND:	03 APPLY:	04 ANALYZE:	05 EVALUATE:	06 CREATE:
Define, Identify, Describe, Recognize, Tell, Explain, Recite, Memorize, Illustrate, Quote	Summarize, Interpret, Classify, Compare, Contrast, Infer, Relate, Extract, Paraphrase, Cite	Solve, Change, Relate, Complete, Use, Sketch, Teach, Articulate, Discover, Transfer	Contrast, Connect, Relate, Devise, Correlate, Illustrate, Distill, Conclude, Categorize, Take Apart	Criticize, Reframe, Judge, Defend, Appraise, Value, Prioritize, Plan, Grade, Reframe	Design, Modify, Role-Play, Develop, Rewrite, Pivot, Modify, Collaborate, Invent, Write

LESSON 6:

SDG: Goal 4. Quality education

(Add as needed)

EVALUATION: Formative (continuous)

Summative (final)

Opospills

UNIT 3:	LESSONS
	LESSON 1:
RESOURCES: (Weblinks of books, videos, songs, games, etc.)	LESSON 2:
	LESSON 3:
DUA: Engagement: Motivation activities Representation: Resources Expression: Final product	LESSON 4:
Cognitive skills: LOTS: HOTS:	LESSON 5:
	LESSON 6:
SDG: Goal 4. Quality education	(Add as needed)
EVALUATION: Formative (continuous) Summative (final)	

Opospills

UNIT 4:	LESSONS
	LESSON 1:
RESOURCES: (Weblinks of books, videos, songs, games, etc.)	LESSON 2:
	LESSON 3:
DUA: Engagement: Motivation activities Representation: Resources Expression: Final product	LESSON 4:
Cognitive skills: LOTS: HOTS:	LESSON 5:

01 KNOWLEDGE Define, Identify, Describe, Recognize, Tell, Explain, Recite, Memorize, Illustrate, Quote	**02 UNDERSTAND:** Summarize, Interpret, Classify, Compare, Contrast, Infer, Relate, Extract, Paraphrase, Cite	**03 APPLY:** Solve, Change, Relate, Complete, Use, Sketch, Teach, Articulate, Discover, Transfer	**04 ANALYZE:** Contrast, Connect, Relate, Devise, Correlate, Illustrate, Distill, Conclude, Categorize, Take Apart	**05 EVALUATE:** Criticize, Reframe, Judge, Defend, Appraise, Value, Prioritize, Plan, Grade, Reframe	**06 CREATE:** Design, Modify, Role-Play, Develop, Rewrite, Pivot, Modify, Collaborate, Invent, Write

	LESSON 6:
SDG: Goal 4. Quality education	(Add as needed)
EVALUATION: Formative (continuous) Summative (final)	

REFERENCES & QUOTATIONS

For case studies

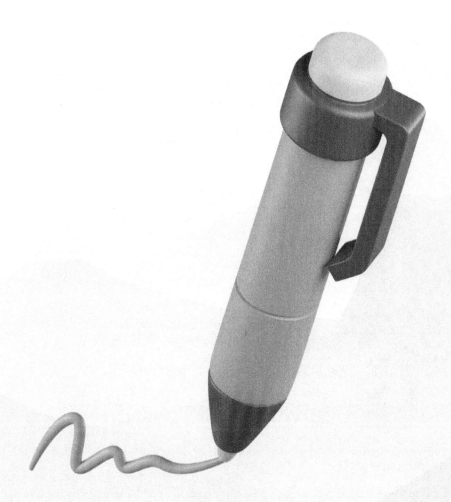

No existen desafíos imposibles,
sino voluntades pequeñas

Opospills

References & quotations
For case studies

Sequence of ideas for the development of case studies

1. Introduction (5 minutes)

- Provide a brief contextualization of the school and the group of students

- Explain the particular situation that you will be addressing in the exam

- Outline the main pedagogical factors that you will be considering

2. Theoretical Framework (15 minutes)

- Present the theoretical framework that informs your teaching practice

- Discuss relevant theories, models, and approaches to language teaching and learning that inform your practice

- Explain how the theoretical framework relates to the practical components of the exam

3. Activities for a group of students (25 minutes)

- Discuss the different types of activities that could be used to address the particular situation

- Provide examples of activities that would be suitable for students with special needs, a mixed-ability class, high ability students, etc.

- Explain how these activities align with the chosen methodology or teaching approach

- Discuss how technology could be used to support the activities, providing examples of specific tools or resources

References & quotations

For case studies

4. Evaluation (10 minutes)

- Discuss how you would evaluate student learning during the process

- Provide examples of formative and summative assessments that could be used

- Explain how you would monitor your own teaching practice and evaluate its effectiveness

- Discuss how student feedback could be used to improve the teaching and learning process

5. Conclusion (5 minutes)

- Summarize the key points made in the exam

- Provide recommendations for next steps

- Explain how the ideas and strategies presented in the exam could be implemented in the classroom

10 Key aspects to include throughout the exam

#1
A clear understanding of the context of the school and the group of students

#2
A detailed explanation of the particular situation being addressed

#3
Connection with the Education legislation, psychological and pedagogical references

#4
Consideration of pedagogical factors such as students with special needs, mixed-ability classes, high ability students, etc

#5
Examples of activities that align with the chosen methodology or teaching approach

#6
Use of technology to support the activities

References & quotations
For case studies

#7
Discussion of how to evaluate student learning and teacher practice

#8
Focus on student-centred learning and differentiated instruction to cater to diversity

#9
Appropriate use of academic language and clear organization

#10
And don't forget the integration of the theoretical framework with the practical components of the exam

Bibliographical references & quotations

The bibliographical references that you include in your exam will depend on the specific theoretical framework and teaching approach that you are focusing on. Here are some examples of references that may be relevant for different theoretical frameworks:

Communicative Language Teaching (CLT) or Communicative Approach

- Canale, M., & Swain, M. (1980). Theoretical bases of communicative approaches to second language teaching and testing. Applied Linguistics, 1(1), 1-47.

- Celce-Murcia, M., et all (2014). Teaching English as a second or foreign language. Heinle

- Larsen-Freeman, D., & Anderson, M. (2011). Techniques and principles in language teaching (3rd ed.). Oxford University Press

- Littlewood, W. (2014). Communicative language teaching: An introduction. Cambridge University Press

- Richards, J. C., & Rodgers, T. S. (2014). Approaches and methods in language teaching. Cambridge University Press

10 Key aspects to include throughout the exam

References & quotations

For case studies

Some quotations supporting these theories:

Larsen-Freeman & Anderson (2011): "The goal of language teaching is to develop communicative competence - the ability to use the language accurately, appropriately, and flexibly to accomplish communication goals in a given context." (p. 2)

Celce-Murcia, Brinton, & Snow (2014): "The communicative approach is built on the belief that language learning is facilitated when learners engage in authentic communication tasks and use language for meaningful purposes." (p. 4)

Canale & Swain (1980): "The ability to communicate effectively in the second language...involves the ability to use the language for a variety of purposes and in a variety of situations." (p. 2)

Action-oriented Approach (AoA)

- Council of Europe. (2018). The CEFR Companion Volume with New Descriptors. Council of Europe

- Little, D. (2011). The Common European Framework of Reference for Languages: Learning, teaching, assessment (CEFR) and the development of language pedagogy. The Language Learning Journal, 39(1), 9-22

- Byram, M., & Wagner, M. (2018). Making the case for the integration of language and culture teaching: The contribution of the Council of Europe's Reference Framework. Language Learning Journal, 46(1), 3-15

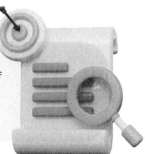

It's important to note that the Action-oriented Approach is heavily influenced by the Common European Framework of Reference for Languages (CEFR), so it may also be useful to reference the CEFR itself and related materials from the Council of Europe

Some quotations:

Council of Europe (2018): "The aim of the CEFR is to describe, in a comprehensive way, what learners have to do in order to use a language for communication purposes, and to provide a set of principles, practices and tools for organizing and evaluating language teaching and learning." (p. 2)

References & quotations

For case studies

Little (2011): "The CEFR has become a key reference point for those involved in the design of materials, syllabuses, curricula, assessment, teacher education and research...It has been an important catalyst for change in the way languages are taught and learned." (p. 16)

Byram & Wagner (2018): "The action-oriented approach aims to teach language and culture together, to integrate teaching of skills with teaching of content, to link the classroom with the wider world, and to enable learners to act effectively in the world they inhabit." (p. 3)

Task-Based Language Teaching (TBLT)

- Ellis, R. (2003). Task-based language learning and teaching. Oxford University Press

- Long, M. H. (2015). Second language acquisition and task-based language teaching. John Wiley & Sons

- Willis, J., & Willis, D. (2007). Doing task-based teaching. Oxford University Press

- Nunan, D. (2004). Task-based language teaching. Cambridge University Press

- Skehan, P. (1996). A framework for the implementation of task-based instruction. Applied Linguistics, 17(1), 38-62

Some quotations:

Willis (1996): "A task is a piece of classroom work which involves learners in comprehending, manipulating, producing, or interacting in the target language while their attention is focused on mobilising their grammatical knowledge in order to express meaning." (p. 2)

Willis and Willis (2007): "In a task-based lesson, the teacher does not pre-determine what language will be studied, the lesson is based around the completion of a central task and the language studied is determined by what happens as the students complete it." (p. 3)

Nunan (2004): "The task-based approach reflects a move away from traditional grammar-based approaches to a more communicative approach... The focus is on enabling learners to use the language in real-life situations, rather than on simply acquiring knowledge about the language." (p. 7)

References & quotations
For case studies

Skehan (1998): "A task-based approach involves the provision of input in the form of tasks, which are related to real-world activities, in order to encourage learners to focus on meaning rather than on form." (p. 89)

Ellis (2003): "Task-based language learning has as its objective the development of a range of abilities associated with the performance of communicative tasks. Such tasks typically involve the acquisition of new information, the manipulation of that information, and the production of a response." (p. 2)

Long (2015): "Task-based language teaching and learning represents an important advance in communicative language teaching...It provides an evidence-based model for syllabus design and materials development." (p. 1)

Content and Language Integrated Learning (CLIL)

- Coyle, D. (2005). Developing CLIL: Towards a theory of practice. University of Maastricht

- Coyle, D., Hood, P., & Marsh, D. (2010). CLIL: Content and language integrated learning. Cambridge University Press

- Dalton-Puffer, C. (2007). Discourse in Content and Language Integrated Learning (CLIL) classrooms. John Benjamins Publishing

- Dalton-Puffer, C. (2011). Content-and-language integrated learning: From practice to principles? Annual Review of Applied Linguistics, 31, 182-204

- Lasagabaster, D., & Sierra, J. M. (2010). Immersion and CLIL in English: More differences than similarities. ELT Journal, 64(4), 367-375

- Marsh, D. (2002). CLIL/EMILE - The European dimension: Actions, trends and foresight potential. European Commission

- Wolff, D., & Marsh, D. (2018). Content and language integrated learning (CLIL) in Europe: Past, present, and future. Bloomsbury Publishing

References & quotations
For case studies

Quotations from CLIL:

Coyle (2005)

"CLIL is a dual-focused educational approach in which an additional language is used for the learning and teaching of both content and language." (p. 2)

"CLIL is a powerful and flexible educational approach that can enable learners to develop both language and cognitive skills in a truly integrated and holistic manner." (p. 51)

Marsh (2002)

"In CLIL the language is not taught as a subject in its own right but is used as a medium of instruction to teach non-language content." (p. 58)

"CLIL is a response to the global demand for multilingual individuals with multicultural competences." (p. 60)

Dalton-Puffer (2007)

"CLIL research focuses on the intersection of language and content learning and on the mutual support which these two dimensions can lend each other in successful L2 acquisition." (p. 1)

"CLIL draws attention to the complementarity of content and language learning." (p. 6)

Wolff and Marsh (2018)

"CLIL can be seen as a bridge between the language classroom and the wider world, offering a powerful and authentic context for language use and development." (p. 10)

"CLIL requires a high degree of integration between the content and the language components of the curriculum, with language and content teachers working closely together to create a coherent and effective learning environment." (p. 13)

Diversity and differentiated Instruction

- Cummins, J. (1984). Bilingualism and special education: Issues in assessment and pedagogy. Multilingual Matters

- Tomlinson, C. A. (2014). The differentiated classroom: Responding to the needs of all learners. ASCD

- Tomlinson, C. A. (2012). How to differentiate instruction in mixed-ability classrooms. ASCD

References & quotations
For case studies

- Tomlinson, C. A. (2017). How to differentiate instruction in academically diverse classrooms. ASCD

- Gregory, G. H., & Chapman, C. (2013). Differentiated instructional strategies: One size doesn't fit all. Corwin

- Nunan, D. (1999). Second language teaching and learning. Heinle & Heinle

- Richards, J. C., & Rodgers, T. S. (2001). Approaches and methods in language teaching. Cambridge University Press

Some quotations are:

Tomlinson (2012)

"Differentiation is a way of teaching that attempts to respond to the diversity of learners in the classroom by adjusting the content, process, or product of learning according to students' learning needs and preferences." (p. 22)

"The aim of differentiation is to enable all students, regardless of their starting point, to make progress in their learning." (p. 24)

Nunan (1999)

"In a diverse classroom, teachers need to recognize and respect the different cultural backgrounds, learning styles, and abilities of their students." (p. 40)

"Teachers can differentiate instruction by using a range of techniques, such as adapting materials, providing extra support or challenge, and allowing for student choice and self-direction." (p. 41)

Cummins (1984)

"Students' academic achievement and language development are closely linked to their cultural and linguistic background, and teachers need to be sensitive to these differences when planning and delivering instruction." (p. 32)

"Differentiation is not just about adjusting the level of difficulty of tasks or materials, but about providing a learning environment that is responsive to the diverse needs and experiences of all students." (p. 34)

References & quotations
For case studies

| **Richards and Rodgers (2001)** | "Teachers can differentiate instruction by providing a range of activities that appeal to different learning styles, such as visual, auditory, or kinesthetic." (p. 193) |
| | "Differentiation can also involve providing opportunities for students to work independently or in groups, and to engage in self-directed or project-based learning." (p. 194) |

Evaluation bibliographical references

- Harlen, W. (2007). Principles and big ideas of assessment for learning. Assessment in Education: Principles, Policy & Practice. Routledge

- Black, P., & Wiliam, D. (1998). Assessment and classroom learning. Assessment in Education: Principles, Policy & Practice. Taylor & Francis

- Shepard, L. A. (2000). The role of assessment in a learning culture. Educational Researcher. American Educational Research Association

- Stiggins, R. J. (2001). The unfulfilled promise of classroom assessment. Educational Measurement: Issues and Practice. Wiley

Some quotations about evaluation:

| **Harlen (2007)** | "Evaluation in primary education should focus on the learning process, not just the end product, and should be based on a range of evidence that reflects the diversity of learners and learning experiences." (p. 12) |
| | "Assessment should be formative, providing feedback that helps students to improve their learning, and should involve students in the process of setting and achieving learning goals." (p. 13) |

| **Black and Wiliam (1998)** | "Assessment should be used to support learning, not just to measure it, and should involve students in reflecting on their own learning and setting goals for improvement." (p. 2) |
| | "Effective assessment in primary education involves a range of methods, including self-assessment, peer assessment, and teacher assessment, and should be integrated into the teaching and learning process." (p. 3) |

References & quotations

For case studies

Shepard (2000)

"Evaluation in primary education should be fair, valid, and reliable, and should reflect the diversity of learners and learning experiences." (p. 90)

"Assessment should be used to support learning, and should involve students in the process of setting and achieving learning goals, as well as monitoring their own progress." (p. 91)

Stiggins (2001)

"Assessment in primary education should be focused on promoting learning, not just measuring it, and should involve students in the process of setting and achieving learning goals." (p. 1)

"Effective assessment involves providing feedback that is clear, specific, and relevant to the learning goals, and that helps students to understand how to improve their learning." (p. 2)

Printed in Great Britain
by Amazon

37800701R00053